LIVERPOOL FC 2013/14 SEASON IN REVIEW: POETRY IN MOTION

This Is Anfield
www.thisisanfield.com

First published worldwide by This Is Anfield, 2014

Text copyright © Karl Matchett, Si Steers, Andrew Lawrence, Neil Poole, Jack Lusby, Henry Jackson, Tom McMahon, Ben Twelves , 2014

Cover photograph © David Rawcliffe, Propaganda, 2014

ISBN 978-1499622614

All rights reserved
This book is sold subject to the condition that it shall not, by way of trade or otherwise, be lent, hired out or otherwise circulated in any form of binding or cover other than that in which it is published. No part of this publication may be reproduced, stored in a retrieval system, or transmitted in any form or by any means (electronic, mechanical, photocopying, recording or otherwise) without the prior written permission of This Is Anfield.

Table of Contents

1. Foreword 5
2. The transformation of Liverpool FC 7
3. Summer transfer window 12
4. That Day at the G 15
5. The 2013-14 Season Begins 20
6. Stoke City 23
7. August - December 28
8. Winter transfer window 40
9. Into the New Year 41
10. The ever-changing tactics of Brendan Rodgers' Liverpool 48
11. End of season run-in 56
12. Best and Worst of 2013-14 65
13. Squad profiles 70
14. Brendan Rodgers in Profile 91
15. Under-21s and under-18s Academy Review 101
16. Liverpool Loan Watch 106
17. LFC Premier League statistics of 2013-14 110

1. Foreword

If 2013-14 was a season where Liverpool just fell short of winning the biggest prize in the English game, it was also a season in which huge strides forward were made as a club, on and off the field. Fans have been privy to some of the best football the team has produce over the last two decades, to stars of youth and prime age and veteran all contributing in sublime and spectacular fashion and to a host of big, confident, deserved beatings handed out to rivals.

Often, especially in recent seasons, looking back at any particular campaign has led fans to be able to pinpoint: that's where we went wrong, here's the transfer we messed up, this is what we should have done.

Liverpool are on a journey, with Brendan Rodgers steering his side toward the glories everybody associated with the club wants to achieve. As much as those in charge have to acknowledge how far there is still to go, how much work yet remains ahead, the fans should be able to take heart and enjoyment from just how far down the road the team has come in a short space of time.

Looking back at a season can sometimes show where a club went wrong, how silverware and success just evaded the players. With a little luck, a lot of work and no shortage of good judgement in the transfer market, a future look back at 2013-14 could instead see fans point out: that's where it all began to go right again.

This is the story of Liverpool's sometimes explosive, often dramatic, perpetually exciting campaign, and how Rodgers and his side made Reds fans dream once more.

Karl Matchett, Editor

2. The transformation of Liverpool FC

By Si Steers

The ending didn't really fit the script of the season but there is no question that Liverpool Football Club has taken a giant stride forward this season. Brendan Rodgers has engineered a side which plays fearless, attacking football that has taken the Reds to within a whisker of the title. We may not quite have gotten over the line, but we have regained our pride, purpose and hope after a few years of drifting through mediocre league campaigns.

There are a number of factors that have all contributed to the transformation at the club, but the majority of the credit has to go to Rodgers and his players for refusing to believe they aren't good enough to compete with clubs that have more money, but less soul.

Liverpool is now very much a club on the rise, but it was just over three years ago that we were a club on our knees, with a second place finish and Champions League football looking like a pipe-dream.

This season has been so refreshing because it has restored belief; it has had supporters daring to dream, looking forward to every game, uniting behind the team and the players.

Enjoying football again.

Football has once again become the dominant conversation; off the field activity has faded into the background—which is where it should be. So what is it this season that has really been the catalyst for that transformation?

The manager

Brendan Rodgers has been outstanding this season, both on the pitch and off it. He is the voice of authority and control, always knowing the right thing to say to the players, supporters and the media. He is a man with his finger on the pulse of his club. At key points in the season he was able to retain his cool, even whilst his more experienced peers looked to unsettle him.

This season's team has been very much built in Rodgers' image: it is full of youth and dynamism, and has ignored the noise from the outside.

The boss has tackled every single obstacle before him in the Liverpool way. He has retained his class, his dignity and, although he is full of belief in his way, is the polar opposite to the egotistical style of somebody like Jose Mourinho.

Rodgers is a Liverpool manager in every sense; he is respectful to our past and our heritage and his nod to Kenny Dalglish during the Hillsborough memorial service was a gesture which removed the focus from him and put it onto the man who guided the club through that tragic period. It was uncomfortable for Dalglish, but it is a sign that Rodgers is a man who knows exactly where this club has come from…and will never lose sight of that.

But the thing that has come to the fore this season, above anything, is that Rodgers has proven himself to be hungry to win, and he has proven beyond question there is substance to his belief and ideas in how he wants the game to be played.

Style of play

We have had some good Liverpool sides since our last league title, but not many that have been as exciting as this one. Liverpool scored 101 league goals in 2013-14; that in turn has left us too exposed, too regularly in a defensive sense, but the ideology of attacking, possession-based football is very much the Liverpool way.

The 5-1 demolition of Arsenal at Anfield was *almost* perfect. It could have easily been more; it was sensational football being played at breakneck speed. When we have been at our best this season, nobody has been able to live with us. Looking at the Crystal Palace game, in some ways it was a microcosm of Liverpool's season—brilliant going forward, but far too open defensively. But take a step back and look at why that was: it had almost everything to do with the desire to score enough goals to put the title destiny back in our own hands, and little to do with what would have happened had it been a "normal" game.

We threw that lead away because we wanted to win by as many goals as possible. That's what this side is built on, scoring goals. It is going to mean that we concede more than some more systematic sides like Chelsea, but under Rodgers we are going to be playing football the Liverpool way.

Liverpool are a genuinely exciting team to watch and it's this change in style, engineered by Rodgers, that has been one of the catalysts to complete transformation at the club.

The supporters

This season has really felt that supporters have reconnected with the club. The scenes around Anfield in the run-in as fans gathered to welcome the team bus were incredible. The atmosphere at Anfield is slowly starting to come back, especially for the big games. European nights next season can only enhance that improvement.

There is an excitement around the club again. When you aren't competing, it is easy as a supporter to spend a lot of time considering why that is the case. But this season, Liverpool supporters have really united behind Rodgers and the team—and the players have responded. The club is being very well run by FSG who are proving that the winning mentality they have put in place at the Red Sox is something they are striving to put in place at Liverpool. Supporters are seeing some of the green shoots of the progress being made off the pitch, with a clear roadmap for Anfield's stadium redevelopment now in play.

The biggest transformation at the club has likely been the restoration of hope for supporters. This season they have been able to dare to dream, and whilst disappointed not to win the title, there is immense pride in how the team have performed, while the consolation of a return to the Champions League has added to the sense of excitement about the future.

The rebirth of Liverpool FC

This season has been transformational because it has seen the rebirth of Liverpool.

It is the start of a new journey, and all of the pieces that make Liverpool FC great are coming together again. We have a manager leading the club that is the essence of class and dignity, we have a style of play that is one of the most attacking and potent in Europe, we have a stable ownership group that are building and encouraging further growth of the club and, at our best, we have the greatest supporters in football.

We have our soul back.

3. Summer transfer window

By Jack Lusby

The 2013 summer transfer window was a frenetic one for Liverpool, with incomings and outgoings aplenty.

The summer began with the retirement of a Liverpool legend—and a dependable defensive stalwart—in Jamie Carragher; with that in mind, the club's first signing of the window was the acquisition of Ivorian international Kolo Toure from Manchester City on a Bosman free transfer, with his new manager hailing his "experience".

This was followed by a further pair of defensive reinforcements aimed more at the future of the club: Portuguese centre-back Tiago Ilori, signed for £7 million from Sporting Lisbon, and French international Mamadou Sakho, who arrived for £18 million from Ligue 1 champions Paris Saint-Germain. Brendan Rodgers further adapted Liverpool's defensive makeup by signing Belgian shot-stopper Simon Mignolet from Sunderland for a fee of £9 million. In order to flesh out a wafer-thin squad, Liverpool brought in Spaniards Luis Alberto and Iago Aspas—£6.8 million from Sevilla and £7 million from Celta Vigo respectively—as well as the loan signings of forward Victor Moses from Chelsea and left-back Aly Cissokho from Valencia.

In terms of more high-profile recruits, the summer transfer window was a disappointing affair. Long-running interests in attacking midfielders Willian and Henrikh Mkhitaryan were both thwarted, with the pair eventually signing for Chelsea and Borussia Dortmund respectively.

However, by far the most agonising transfer saga of the summer was the protracted flirtation of Luis Suarez with a move away from Merseyside—with Arsenal, of all clubs, the most likely suitors. A risible £40 million-plus-£1 bid from the North London club was laughed off by owner John Henry, before the Uruguayan eventually signed a new long-term deal with the club in the autumn.

With a number of permanent outgoings, the Reds kept themselves busy over the summer between confirming new arrivals.

The most high-profile sales saw Jonjo Shelvey leave for £6 million to Swansea City, Andy Carroll made his move to West Ham United permanent for £15 million, Stewart Downing followed him for £6 million and Jay Spearing dropped to the Championship, moving to Bolton Wanderers for £1.7 million.

Elsewhere, Dani Pacheco (Alcorcon), Peter Gulacsi (Red Bull Salzburg) and Danny Wilson (Hearts) also all left for pastures new on free transfers.

As well as the two incoming loans, Rodgers utilised the temporary market wisely to gift a number of his peripheral figures valuable game time. Suso headed to Spain's top flight for a season with Almeria, Fabio Borini made a Premier League switch to Sunderland and Andre Wisdom headed for the

Championship with Derby County. Having impressed to varying degrees, all three can likely look forward to next season with the Reds with a renewed vigour.

Elsewhere, Pepe Reina (Napoli), Jack Robinson (Blackpool), Conor Coady (Sheffield United) and Oussama Assaidi (Stoke City) will all have put themselves in the shop window with their performances on loan.

4. That Day at the G

By Andrew Lawrence

The Melbourne Cricket Ground (MCG) holds a special place in the heart of sports-loving Melbournians. Like the Eiffel Tower, Big Ben or Tower Bridge, the Colosseum, or Statue of Liberty, this grand old stadium is an historical monument that helps define our city. Unlike the other landmarks though, the MCG is not just a cultural icon or tourist attraction, but an integral part of our daily existence; a sporting mecca for all those who love to watch grown men or women kick, throw, hit, punch or head-butt a ball of any size.

Coming to play out an event in a city that hosts one of only four tennis Grand Slams, the world's second-richest horse race (The Melbourne Cup) and a Formula One Grand Prix event, or coming to a ground that has hosted an Olympic Games, Commonwealth Games, cricket, rugby union, rugby league, Australian Rules Football (our indigenous football code one English friend once described as aerial ping pong) and 'the beautiful game' in many of its guises, including international friendlies and World Cup qualifiers, it's not easy to impose yourself on the local sporting consciousness.

However, when Liverpool Football Club ventured down under as part of the 2013-14 preseason tour it managed just that, and etched itself into the history of one of the world's greatest sporting stadiums in the process.

If the crowd of 95,446 wasn't impressive enough for a friendly match (and the second-highest 'soccer' crowd at the stadium in history, behind only the 104,700 who witnessed the 1956 Olympic Games Final between the USSR and Yugoslavia) then *that* rendition of "You'll Never Walk Alone" is sure to remain firmly established in the memory banks of all those who witnessed it.

Before that moment my only real memory of organised song-singing at the MCG occurred when I was 14, and had made my first foray into this sporting Disneyland via the infamous Bay 13. The only game in town that summer was the 1982 Ashes test match against the old enemy, England. Apart from the banter, the crowd and the spectacle, my lasting memory of the day was the realisation that it was possible for a group of grown men to chant "get your top off" to a buxom lass and receive an unexpected response in the affirmative.

Over several decades the ground has treated me to a who's who of cricket greatness. It's treated me to the Windies at their peak. Lillee, Thompson, Botham, Hadlee and McGrath. A pig with 'Gatting' scribbled on the side.

There have been Australian Football League (AFL) Grand Finals including one of the greatest in living memory: a 1989 match in which my team's star player was deliberately poleaxed at the opening whistle, in attempt to remove him from the game. Stretchered off the ground with broken ribs, a bruised kidney and internal bleeding, he returned to the ground to inspire a memorable victory.

There has been the pain of the Socceroos traumatic 1997 World

Cup qualifying tie with Iran, when a rampant Mark Viduka and Harry Kewell were stopped in their tracks by a serial pest (who also disrupted the funeral of INXS front man Michael Hutchence and numerous other events). When that fool ran onto the ground and pulled down the goal nets, he prolonged a nations 24-year wait for a World Cup appearance in the process.

In all that time though, I've never witnessed anything close to that song, to the sheer improbability of it all. Australia might share some of its origins with England, and enjoy the same banter, but when it comes to singing at football matches, well, quite simply, we don't.

At the cricket, the best the crowd can muster is generally something idiotic like that annoying "Aussie, Aussie, Aussie, Oi, Oi, Oi" nonsense. The Australian Football League (AFL) has cheer squads who raise the occasional chant, but they are generally viewed by the rest of us with a mixture of bemusement and pity. When national teams play, the national anthem 'Advance Australia Fair' might get belted out by a few that love the sound of their own voice, and mumbled along by a slice of the rest (many of whom, despite our Federal government's educational efforts, still can't remember all the words), but a significant portion always remains notably silent.

This is not to say that there is no noise at the 'G.

The ground is a famous one for a reason. There is always atmosphere. However, what we Australians don't do is sing en masse. When the MCG crowd launched into the mandatory rendition of "You'll Never Walk Alone" on July 24, 2013, what made the moment so special was the sheer universality of it. *Everyone* sang. From the Great Southern Stand to the MCC Members, from the Olympic Stand to the Ponsford. The crowd sang as one.

95,000 people belted out a Gerry and the Pacemakers classic with hardly a passenger. To those who have watched England play at Wembley, or have a season ticket at Anfield, that might not seem like a big deal, but in Australia that is unheard of. It just doesn't happen. So impressive was that moment that football sceptics and soccer haters were wandering the streets of Melbourne for days afterwards in awe. A colleague of mine played a recording for me on his phone. He doesn't really like soccer, but *what about that, aye?*

YouTube doesn't really do it justice.

For me though, more memorable than the song, was the colour. The mass of Red from the top tier to the ground ringed the complete circle of the stadium, including the traditionally more conservative members' area. When Australia plays there are always pockets of gold and green, and sometimes a long glimmer of colour throughout the stadium, but nothing like that. Nothing that comprehensive. Nothing so emphatic, so unifying.

When Liverpool Football Club announced after the game that it had broken the club's single-day merchandising record it was hardly a surprise. What was surprising was that it had taken the club so long to make its inaugural trip to this great southern land. When Reds fans look back at the 2013-14 season and reflect on a campaign that promises so much for the future, perhaps the biggest source of optimism should be the manner in which the club showed it is finally awakening to the financial possibilities beyond its traditional shores. If this off-field success can translate into more on-field resources...well, that is something truly worth getting excited about.

Liverpool's summer preseason friendly results

July 13: 4-0 vs Preston North End (Deepdale) - Coutinho (pen), Ibe, Sterling, Aspas

July 20: 2-0 vs Indonesia XI (GBK Stadium) - Coutinho, Sterling

July 24: 2-0 vs Melbourne Victory (Melbourne Cricket Ground) - Gerrard, Aspas

July 28: 3-0 vs Thailand (National Stadium, Bangkok) - Coutinho, Aspas, Gerrard

August 3: 2-0 vs Olympiacos (Anfield, Steven Gerrard Testimonial) - Allen, Henderson

August 7: 4-1 vs Valerenga (Ullevaal Stadium, Oslo) - Luis Alberto, Aspas, Kelly, Sterling

August 10: 0-1 vs Celtic (Aviva Stadium, Dublin) - n/a

5. The 2013-14 Season Begins

By Karl Matchett

August, 2013

Liverpool have opened their competitive calendar with a European fixture in six out of the last nine seasons, but with no continental football on offer for Brendan Rodgers' charges in 2013-14 it was straight into the Premier League in mid-August this time around.

A lack of European action also meant one other change to the early-season schedule: along with two tough league games, the Reds would start with a League Cup second round fixture, one round earlier in the domestic cup than usual.

With the transfer window of course still open by the time the new season kicked off, there was still an element of uncertainty and expectation around the shape of the squad, with four early summer transfer deals not having been added to by the time the Reds took the field competitively for the first time.

It has often been a cause of complaint for some supporters that the Reds get a tough opening to the fixture list, but for the third time in four seasons Liverpool opened their league campaign with a match at Anfield. It was to be a happy occasion too; not since 2008-09 had Liverpool managed to taste victory on the opening day, but Stoke City were beaten 1-0 on August 17 to get the Reds off to a flyer—not that the match was without the odd moment of heart-in-mouth situations, of course.

Rodgers selected a new central defensive pairing of Kolo Toure and Daniel Agger to start the season, while Daniel Sturridge was supported by new signing Iago Aspas in attack. There were plenty of attacking options on the bench with the likes of Jordon Ibe, Luis Alberto and Fabio Borini to call on, but it was Sturridge who scored the only goal of the game with a low, driven strike from 20 yards.

Throughout the game the better chances fell Liverpool's way, but they were unable to score the second goal to kill the game off and Stoke went close themselves with a handful of chances.

Right at the last, it looked as though the points had been squandered in the 90th minute when Daniel Agger conceded a penalty from a hand-ball.

Debutant goalkeeper Simon Mignolet, however, pulled off a fantastic double save, denying Jon Walters from the spot with a dive low to his right and then bounding up to block the rebound effort from Kenwyne Jones.

The cheers from the stands which greeted the double stop—and the ensuing clearance from the subsequent corner—were every bit as loud as those which had greeted Sturridge's first-half goal.

After the game Rodgers praised Sturridge's work-rate in the off season to work his way back to fitness after injury, while Mignolet admitted his last-minute penalty save was "the debut you dream of." Given that the fixture was the early kick-off on the opening day it also left the Reds top of the table—something Rodgers joked in pointing out in his post-match press conference.

Little did he know what the season ahead would hold in store in that regard...

6. Stoke City

By Neil Poole

After dominating the opening game of the season, Liverpool were delivered a cruel sucker punch when Jonathan Walters' 87th-minute equaliser from the penalty spot earned Stoke City an unlikely point...

Wait there! That didn't happen. Sling your hook, fictitious parallel world based on four years of opening-day disappointment!

No siree! The very first 90 minutes of the best season for years didn't care that it was rude to point and instead defiantly directed a straight index finger at the remaining 37 games. It turned to the Anfield faithful and said, "I've had it with this two steps forward, three steps back nonsense. This season is going to be *different*."

Liverpool 1. Stoke City 0.

It was so important. Liverpool's one-nil victory over Stoke was the Reds' first opening day win since they'd beaten Sunderland by the same scoreline at the Stadium of Light in 2008; a season in which the Reds also went on to finish second. To give an idea how many worlds away that was from August 2013, let's put that into some context:

Liverpool's goal scorer, Fernando Torres, was one of the best strikers in Europe and a man who was so loved that even the most exercise-adverse of Kopites would gladly bounce to his song. Damien Plessis started the game. You're doing better than most if you can even picture his face. And people were kidding themselves that new recruit Robbie Keane would be the final piece in the jigsaw.

Two words: flatter, deceive.

Since that game in 2008 Rafa has gone. Hodgson and Dalglish have both been and gone, too. An opening day 2-1 defeat away to Spurs in 2009 and a deflating 3-0 reverse to West Brom in 2012…they've been and gone also.

Liverpool led 1-0 at Anfield to Arsenal and Sunderland in the 2010 and 2011 curtain raisers arrived—but both potential victories disappeared in the aftermath of avoidable equalisers.

That's a whole lot of *gone*.

It was horribly symbolic of the whereabouts of the enthusiasm, enjoyment and hope amongst many Liverpool supporters after four years of drudgery, a couple of cup finals aside.

So, on the first day of the 2013-14 season there was wisdom in the masses. Simon Mignolet's double save from Walters' late penalty summoned a roar worthy of two goals from an Anfield faithful that knew that the momentum from the second half of the previous campaign could easily and immediately be lost if the team stumbled out of the blocks. Not only were there early signs that the progress on the pitch was going to be cranked up several gears, but this was going to be season when the malaise seeped away and the crowd would find its true voice again.

Many of the reasons for this rediscovery of a love affair were on show at the Stoke game; a veritable buffet of bite-sized appetisers for what would unfold in the season ahead.

The devastating accuracy of Gerrard's set pieces—which would prove particularly important in the second half of the season—were evident on the typically sunny August opener. Only a close offside call prevented Daniel Sturridge from opening his account early on as he headed home Gerrard's pinpoint free-kick from the right of the 18 yard box; a feature throughout the season, not least in the final game when Liverpool scored two against Newcastle in quick succession from this same set piece routine.

Later on in the first half against Stoke, Sturridge got the vital goal to secure the 3 points, as he would many times during the season. If fans didn't know it already, it was soon made abundantly clear that they had another match-winner on their hands despite the absence of the peckish Luis Suarez. Unlike in previous seasons in Liverpool's modern history, they now had more than one player who could be relied upon to score the crucial goals. His drive from 20 yards out funnelled through the legs of Robert Huth and nestled in the bottom right corner. It was a tip of the hat to the host of cheeky and brilliant goals which would see the No. 15 leave the likes of Everton and West Bromwich Albion embarrassed throughout the campaign.

Elsewhere, the prominent role that Jordan Henderson would play throughout the season was there for all to see, as he was denied almost-certain goals by first the woodwork and then a great save from Asmir Begovic. These efforts didn't pre-empt a prolific goal scoring season, but his all-action display and involvement at the forefront of everything was symbolic of the way he would be impossible to ignore and become integral to Liverpool's play as the season unfolded.

Liverpool may have only scored one goal but the fact that Begovic was the busiest man on the pitch shone an early light on the season ahead, where the side would pepper the opposition's goal and keepers across the country would regularly claim for overtime expenses in the wake of facing the mighty Reds.

And then, there was the sheer drama, the nervous tension and the raw emotion that would colour the season.

This was a 38 game stretch which would see Gerrard wear his heart on his sleeve like never before. His crazed, staring eyed celebrations against Everton and Fulham, his barely concealed tears against Manchester City and his desolation against Chelsea were all just a continuation of his response to Mignolet's penalty save on that first day. The scream in the face and a punch on the arm afforded to Liverpool's goalie demonstrated that Gerrard was wound up tightly and ready to spring into action over the course of the season.

All of Gerrard's reactions to the delightful and agonising mayhem of the season would be echoed 45,000 fold by the supporters in the stands.

Yes, it was all there from the start. The stagnation of the previous four seasons was left behind as Liverpool collectively popped the cork on the bottle, let the champagne out and celebrated the avoidance of predictable regressions. Instead, this was a season for gleefully volatile progression.

7. August - December

By Karl Matchett

Those three points secured against Stoke gave Liverpool a good start to the season, but a start was all it was, and attentions quickly turned to their first away game, at Aston Villa.

The same XI began the game, though a new addition to the bench was loan signing Aly Cissokho, who came on to make his debut for the Reds in the second half.

At Villa Park, fans saw two faces of the team; the first half was all about the Reds' interplay and movement in attack, while the second needed a much more resolute, defensive display. The season's opening game repeated itself as Sturridge scored—a sublime individual goal of skill and composure this time—and Mignolet again called upon to make some outstanding saves.

Rodgers again paid tribute to his stopper: "You always say a good 'keeper saves you 10 points a season. Last week [vs Stoke] he saved two with the penalty save, here he's made a terrific save at the end so…he's up to four already."

The final match in August saw Liverpool host League One side Notts County in the Capital One Cup second round. A host of changes were made to the starting XI as the likes of Cissokho, Andre Wisdom, Luis Alberto, Ibe and Sterling all started, and by half-time the Reds were 2-0 up and cruising thanks to goals from Sterling and Sturridge, but their opponents scored two in the second half—the equaliser coming six minutes from the end—to send the tie to extra time.

Undeterred, the Reds went again in the added 30 minutes and fine solo goals from Sturridge and Jordan Henderson gave them a 4-2 win on the night, and passage into the third round.

September, 2013

The Reds' third league game of the season saw Manchester United, no longer under the tyrannic rule of Alex Ferguson, visit Anfield. Though the fixture itself always provides a tense atmosphere and the expectation of a close game, in truth Liverpool were comfortably better than their rivals and didn't often look like surrendering their early lead, even when United had more possession in the second half.

The final score had a familiar look about it: 1-0 to Liverpool, Daniel Sturridge the scorer and Simon Mignolet having made a handful of impressive saves. Sturridge scored inside the first five minutes, flicking in a header from close range after Daniel Agger had nodded a corner kick his way.

Rodgers was asked, at the final whistle, whether the three-game winning run at the start of the season heralded a title-chase was on; he replied exactly as you'd expect: "We won't be getting carried away. The initial challenge is to get into the top four."

The wisdom of his words, seemingly, were proven in the next game; Liverpool conceded early on to former midfielder Jonjo Shelvey in an away match at Swansea City, only for Sturridge to level straight away. Debutant Victor Moses scored just past the half-hour mark to give the Reds a half-time lead, but Michu's equaliser meant the side dropped points for the first time in 2013-14. Shelvey was involved in all four goals in the match, showing both the best and worst of his game which Liverpool fans had witnessed the previous season.

Mamadou Sakho also made his Liverpool debut in the match, immediately splitting opinion over whether he had had a good initial impact or was to blame for Swansea's goals. Andre Wisdom, meanwhile, made his first league start of the campaign, with Glen Johnson absent.

Back at Anfield, Liverpool suffered their first defeat of the season as they went down 1-0 to Southampton. Rodgers went with a back four comprised entirely of central defenders, asking Kolo Toure and Mamadou Sakho to provide a solid platform on either flank, but it didn't really work out for the Reds who were blunted in attack and starved of possession. Dejan Lovren scored a header from a corner, a weakness of the Reds side for too long, and Simon Mignolet had to make more difficult saves than Artur Boruc did at the other end to keep the score 1-0.

Worse was to follow in the midweek cup clash. Liverpool were up against Manchester United again, this time in the Capital One Cup third round, and suffered a second consecutive 1-0 defeat after Javier Hernandez's goal at the start of the second half. The match marked the return to first-team action of Luis Suarez after he served out the remainder of his suspension from the previous campaign, and he hit the crossbar with a free-kick in the closest

Liverpool came to an equaliser.

Liverpool got back to winning ways after that three-match slump, with a 3-1 win at Sunderland. It was the first league game that the SAS—Luis Suarez and Daniel Sturridge—front line partnership was renewed for, and those two tore into the Black Cats' defence repetitively and relentlessly.

Manager Rodgers operated with a three-man defence, employing Jose Enrique and Jordan Henderson as wing-backs, as he sought to pair the duo centrally.

Martin Skrtel had an early goal ruled out for offside and Seb Larsson hit the woodwork for Sunderland, before Sturridge headed home from a corner to put the Reds ahead. Sturridge then turned provider as he set up a brace for Suarez to finish from close range. Emanuele Giaccherini scored in between the two from the No. 7, but the Reds were not to be denied and moved back to second place in the early league table by the end of September.

October, 2013

With no European football and having been knocked out of the Capital One Cup, Liverpool's October programme was significantly reduced: they played just three times that month, twice at home in the league and once away.

Crystal Palace were first up at Anfield, where a first-half performance blew the London side away. Suarez and Sturridge both scored, the latter from an acute angle after a determined solo run, before Raheem Sterling won a penalty which Steven Gerrard dispatched.

Victor Moses also managed to hit the crossbar from just a yard out, while at the other end Mamadou Sakho almost put through his own net. Despite the impressive half-time lead, Liverpool didn't dominate play or take their chances after the break, with the score ending 3-1 after Dwight Gayle scored a neat header. Brendan Rodgers was justifiably cautious in his post-match speech as a result: "The front two were outstanding, but behind them we have a lot of work to do. Our loss of control was especially disappointing."

Travelling to Newcastle United is often a fixture which has seen the Reds show some of their best form, but they found it difficult going against the Magpies this time around. Yohan Cabaye's spectacular long-range effort put the home side ahead and the Reds didn't create much in reply, at least until Suarez was pulled down in the box by Mapou Yanga-Mbiwa. The defender was sent off and Gerrard scored the resulting penalty, tying the match before the break, but shortly afterward Newcastle went ahead again as Paul Dummett was left unmarked to score his first senior goal.

Suarez drove down the left and crossed for Sturridge to head in an equaliser for 2-2, before smashing the crossbar himself with a ferocious volley late on, but it always looked like an uphill struggle for the Reds on the day. There were two centuries of note: Gerrard's penalty was his 100th league goal, while Suarez played his 100th game for the club, scoring his 54th goal in the process.

Rodgers was adamant his side were heading in the right direction despite failing to win against ten men. "I still think there is a hell of a lot of improvement for us...the money we have spent is nowhere near the top four or five but we are here to compete. We are never happy when we don't win, but we have to have a sense of perspective as well."

Perspective, of course, cuts both ways, and some fans might have needed it for the opposite reason after the next game—a thumping 4-1 home victory over West Bromwich Albion at Anfield. Luis Suarez was at his irresistible best as he spanked a hat-trick past the Baggies: a solo run (complete with trademark nutmeg) and finish, a 20-yard header into the top corner and a glancing effort to divert a free kick home. That took the Uruguayan to six league goals in four games since his return from suspension.

Lucas Leiva gave away a dubious-looking penalty, dispatched by James Morrison for 3-1, before Sturridge served up the goal of the game with a fantastic chipped effort from range, over the 'keeper and into the far corner of the net.

Meanwhile, Martin Kelly came on as substitute for his first league appearance of the season after a long-term injury, while former Reds assistant Steve Clarke—at the time the West Brom manager—paid to tribute to his old club. "Some days you need to hold your hands up and say the best team won. When you look at the strikers around the world, [Suarez] is certainly in the top five."

The three points meant Liverpool ended October in third place, with six wins and 20 points from nine games, two points off leaders Arsenal.

November, 2013

Speaking of the Gunners, they were Liverpool's next opponents at the beginning of a exciting-looking month.

The Reds went to the Emirates knowing a win would see them leapfrog Arsenal, but they struggled to impose themselves on the match at all and suffered a deserved 2-0 defeat on the day. Rodgers changed his 3-5-2 to a 4-2-3-1 at the break, with Philippe Coutinho returning from injury to aid the switch at half-time, but even he couldn't help the Reds hit top form as Santi Cazorla and Aaron Ramsey scored the goals, with Arsenal's midfield overwhelming that of Liverpool's.

The manager admitted the Reds were second best, though indicated the outcome could have been rather different if they had managed to take one of the chances they created before Ramsey's telling strike.

Back at Anfield for the next game, Rodgers opted to abandon the back-three system and, with a more packed midfield, saw captain Steven Gerrard utterly dominate Fulham.

The No. 8 was involved in all four goals, sending over set pieces for the opening two, humiliating Dimitar Berbatov in the buildup for the third and claiming another assist for the last. An own goal from Fernando Amorebieta, a Martin Skrtel header and another brace for Suarez—eight in six games now—saw the game end 4-0 as Liverpool returned to winning ways in style.

Jose Enrique returned to the team after injury and praised Gerrard's impact, also joking that the skipper would be able to be doing the same job of delivering great set pieces and passes when he reached 50 years of age! Rodgers, meanwhile, was pleased his team showed signs of developing a ruthless streak: "When I first came here there was a nervousness, a vulnerability about the group when it came to these types of games, but we are becoming relentless."

Liverpool's next challenge would be one that every fan looked forward to when the fixture lists came out each summer: the first Merseyside derby of the season, and a short away trip to Everton.

It turned out to be one for the ages, a classic derby encounter in which both sides led, both looked to attack at every opportunity and, somehow, nobody was sent-off in. That latter statistic was severely put to the test when Kevin Mirallas almost took Suarez's leg off at the knee, but the Belgian was only booked for his dangerous foul. The Reds' best performer on the day was perhaps Scouse full-back Jon Flanagan, playing at left-back, but his contribution was easily overlooked due to all the goals flying in.

From start to finish, it was all happening at both ends.

Chances came and went, big saves were made by both Mignolet and Tim Howard, while Philippe Coutinho netted his first league goal of the season to open the scoring. Mirallas equalised from close range before a terrific low free-kick from Suarez put the Reds back ahead before half-time.

Considering the forward had only recently returned from international duty before the game, involving long-haul flights to Jordan and back from Uruguay, he put in another tireless and excellent performance for the side, leading Steven Gerrard to label him a "machine" after the game. There was still a second half to get through, though, and Liverpool looked as though they had let the points slip away late on. Joe Allen missed a fantastic chance to make it 3-1, before a Romelu Lukaku brace in 10 minutes put the blue half of the city ahead, with the clock having already ticked past the 80th minute. It was left to substitute Daniel Sturridge to leap and glance home a header in the last minute of the game to rescue an epic 3-3 draw.

Rodgers best summed up the game with the first word of his post-match press conference: "Wow."

One each of a win, a draw and a defeat in November meant the Reds ended the month in second place, six points behind leaders Arsenal but having played a game less, and level on points with Chelsea and Everton, both behind the Reds on goal difference.

December, 2013

December proved an exceptionally busy month for Liverpool as always, with no less than seven league games for the first team to attend to.

The month didn't get off to the best of starts as the Reds lost 3-1 at Hull City in what was perhaps their worst 90-minute performance of the entire campaign. Steven Gerrard whipped in a free-kick to equalise after a deflected opener, but the home side scored twice in the final 20 minutes after some sloppy defensive work from Liverpool, culminating in a Martin Skrtel own goal at the death.

Thankfully, Norwich City were next up: Luis Suarez's favourite opposition, and at Anfield to boot.

Pre-match jokes centred around the "guaranteed" hat-trick for the No. 7 whenever he takes on the Canaries; by full-time he had risen the bar even higher as the Uruguayan tore into Norwich relentlessly and ended up with four goals of his own, plus an assist for Raheem Sterling, in a 5-1 victory. At least two of Suarez's were goal of the season contenders, while he took his personal tally to 13 in nine league games as a result.

With his third goal, Suarez set a new club record of netting a hat-trick against the same opposition three times.

There was no time to sit back and admire his achievements though; the Reds were at home to West Ham United just three days later, eager to crack on with another winning run.

They did exactly that by putting four past the Hammers, with Mamadou Sakho scoring his first goal for the club and Suarez hitting another two late goals. Guy Demel scored an own goal for the game's opener, while Skrtel matched the right-back's achievements with another own goal of his own to leave the final score at 4-1.

One of the biggest tests of Liverpool's top-four credentials was to come next, with a trip to White Hart Lane to play Tottenham Hotspur. Spurs, under Andre Villas-Boas' guidance, were seen as a direct rival for Liverpool's Champions League hopes—but by the end of the match, there was little doubt about which team were better-equipped for that particular challenge. The Reds produced perhaps the most accomplished all-round away performance of the Premier League season to humiliate Spurs 5-0 in front of their own fans, showing both defensive aggression and attacking menace throughout the 90 minutes.

Jordan Henderson provided Suarez with an assist for the first goal, before the same two were involved for the second, the midfielder netting this time. Paulinho was then sent-off for a kick which caught Suarez in the chest, before Jon Flanagan embarked on an emotional, semi-hysterical celebration after slamming his first club goal in off the crossbar for 3-0.

Suarez lobbed in a fourth and then set up Sterling for a fifth, on a day of great celebration and excitement for Liverpool fans. Rodgers claimed his side were like "animals without the ball" due to their pressing and determination to win the ball back quickly; it was to be an indication of what was to come over the second half of the season.

A 3-1 home win over Cardiff City followed, as Liverpool ended up on top of the league table over Christmas. Suarez scored either side of another Sterling strike, all the goals coming in the first half, before Cardiff scored off a set piece after the break.

As pleasing as the results had been in December up until that point, the Reds faced their two biggest challenges of the season in succession thereafter, and fell just short against Manchester City and Chelsea. Brendan Rodgers' charges were excellent at the Etihad, but missed a shed-load of chances to score a second goal. Philippe Coutinho did open the scoring, but a Vincent Kompany header and a strike from Alvaro Negredo which Mignolet couldn't quite keep out led to a 2-1 defeat for Liverpool. At Chelsea it was rather different; the home side were clearly the fresher side, able to make more changes during the busy festive period and deservedly beat Liverpool in the end, though again, the Reds initially took the lead—Skrtel scoring at the right end this time—before an Eden Hazard-inspired Chelsea fought back to win 2-1.

Those two defeats meant Liverpool ended 2013 in fifth place, one point behind rivals Everton in fourth and six points adrift of league leaders Arsenal. They did, however, have a two-point buffer down to Manchester United and Spurs below them.

8. Winter transfer window

By Henry Jackson

The January transfer window always brings with it an imbalanced ratio of rumours and expectation to actual time and likelihood of completing deals, but even so, Reds fans were made to suffer through more sagas than they would have liked—especially with no ultimate end product.

Liverpool went on rather public chases of two wingers: Egyptian Mohamed Salah and Ukrainian Yevhen Konoplyanka. The former ended up signing for Chelsea from FC Basel, while Konoplynaka did not leave his club at all; ultimately, it transpired that Dnipro Dnipropetrovsk's owner simply refused to do business and sign the documents to release the wide attacker, meaning the Reds ended the month empty handed.

There was little outgoing transfer activity either, with just a clutch of younger players heading out on loan for what was left of the season. Jordon Ibe, Ryan McLaughlin and Tiago Ilori all headed out during January to Birmingham City, Barnsley and Spanish side Granada respectively, while striker Adam Morgan made his loan move to Yeovil a permanent one. The other most notable deal was Uruguayan defender Sebastian Coates heading to his former club Nacional, as he bid to both recover from his long-term injury and gain some important match time in a World Cup year.

9. Into the New Year

By Karl Matchett

January, 2014

The new year brought not only a chance to bounce back to winning ways in the league, but also further domestic cup fixtures with the beginning of Liverpool's involvement in the FA Cup. Of course, it also brought the opening of the transfer window and another four weeks of speculation, discussion and stress, too.

The first game of the new year saw the Reds make up for their lacklustre performance against Hull in December by beating the same opposition at Anfield, by a 2-0 scoreline. Daniel Agger scored his first of the season with a fine header, before Suarez struck a free-kick to record his 20th of the campaign—in just 15 league matches. Coutinho also added a late third after a fantastic solo run, but was denied by the opposition goalkeeper Alan McGregor.

The likes of Brad Jones, Martin Kelly, Luis Alberto and Victor Moses were all handed starts for the FA Cup third round fixture against Oldham Athletic at Anfield. Sterling created both goals in a 2-0 win, first crossing for Iago Aspas to volley home his only goal of the season and then shooting against James Tarkowski, who put through his own net. Youngsters Tiago Ilori and Cameron Brannagan were both on the bench for the Reds, though neither came on to feature during the game. Brendan Rodgers was forced to make a double change at the break after an uninspiring first half from the Reds against their League One opponents, with Moses and Alberto being withdrawn to "create more speed and intensity" in the game.

A tough away trip to the Britannia Stadium was next up, with away days at Stoke City not usually ones which are relished by the big clubs.

Liverpool strode into an early two-goal lead thanks to Aly Cissokho's deflected shot and a Luis Suarez goal—both saw errors by Ryan Shawcross—before former Reds Peter Crouch and Charlie Adam got Stoke back on level terms before half-time. A crazy, memorable second half ensued, with Steven Gerrard converting a penalty and Suarez notching a second to restore the two-goal advantage, before Mignolet failed to keep out a Jon Walters effort late on to make it 4-3. Daniel Sturridge, on as substitute in the second half, brilliantly beat Jack Butland at the second attempt late on in the game, thus wrapping up an eventual 5-3 victory for Liverpool.

The season had had its ups and downs by that point, of course, but few would contest the notion that as a whole, 2013-14 had so far been largely impressive as far as Liverpool were concerned. Following the win over Stoke they were back in the top four and only five points off the top, with an almost perfect home record: nine wins and one defeat from 10 games.

That made the next game all the more surprising; the Reds faced Aston Villa at Anfield, with the away side in mid-table but only five points above an extremely tight and congested relegation zone—six points separated 10th from 20th at that point.

A change of tactics for the game and a slow start from the Reds made it all go horribly pear-shaped early on, and Villa were deservedly 2-0 up after little more than half an hour of play. The Reds were cut open down both defensive channels in the first half, lacked protection in front of the defence and had little meaningful possession, so a Sturridge goal in the seconds before half-time was a welcome sight. Steven Gerrard netted a penalty after the break to level the scores, but it was a game Liverpool rarely looked like taking three points from and they had to settle for a 2-2 draw.

Back in the FA Cup, the Reds then faced AFC Bournemouth in the fourth round. A low Victor Moses drive put the Reds ahead and, despite not always having it their own way against their Championship opponents, saw out the game to win 2-0 after Sturridge netted another on the hour mark.

The final game of January for Liverpool was the second Merseyside derby of the campaign, and a memorable Tuesday evening for everybody in Red.

Liverpool didn't just set out to beat Everton, they tore into them once more from the start with what was fast becoming a team trademark; great aggression off the ball, fast transitions and a clinical edge in the final third.

Steven Gerrard scored a header from a corner after 21 minutes and the team didn't look back.

Sturridge's constant runs off the ball were giving Everton all sorts of problems, and when first Coutinho and then Kolo Toure found him down the middle with intelligent through passes, Sturridge beat Tim Howard twice in three minutes to treble Liverpool's lead.

Luis Suarez scored his 23rd league goal of the season shortly after half-time after embarking on a determined run from the halfway line, to give Liverpool a 4-0 win. It could have been even more, but Sturridge spurned his hat-trick chance by blazing a penalty over the bar and into the Kop.

February, 2014

After having beaten Everton in such accomplished fashion, West Bromwich Albion were not expected to hold too many problems for Liverpool—and so that would have been the case, but not for a misplaced pass.

The Reds weren't at their best, true, but they still led 1-0 past the hour mark after a first-half Sturridge goal, his 14th of the league season. Liverpool looked comfortable and in control, despite missing a few chances, but Kolo Toure's inexplicable square ball across his penalty area gifted Victor Anichebe a cheap equaliser. Unable to raise their game thereafter, the Reds had to settle for a point from the 1-1 draw.

A week to reflect on that game came before the next: a home fixture against top-four rivals Arsenal—a game which sparked Liverpool's amazing 10-week run of form and genuine, believable talk of a title bid.

Like Tottenham, like Everton, Arsenal were simply blown away by Liverpool's relentless pressing, aggression and speed going forward. The Gunners were top of the table and eight points clear of Liverpool going into the game; by the end of it they were off the summit, their goal difference had taken a hammering and confidence looked shot. Liverpool were the complete opposite—they'd shown themselves, as much as anyone else, that they could not only compete against the best in the league, but also beat them convincingly.

Martin Skrtel scored twice off set pieces in the opening 10 minutes, Raheem Sterling scored off a low cross from the right and Daniel Sturridge side-footed home a fourth—all within a spectacular opening 20 minutes. Luis Suarez almost broke the goal frame with an outrageous volley from distance, while Kolo Toure missed an almost open goal from the rebound. Sterling added a fifth after half-time as Liverpool finally relented somewhat, with a penalty for Arsenal proving pitiful, immaterial consolation.

Gerrard and Rodgers remained aloof from title talk after the game, but the captain left no doubts about just how good the performance was: "That's as explosive as it gets. That is right up there, in the top three performances I've been involved in. We absolutely demolished a top team there from start to finish."

Not every game, of course, could be as much of a rampant victory as that one proved to be, as Fulham reminded Liverpool of just a few days later. The Reds went to Craven Cottage with their morale well and truly lifted, but some horrendous moments of defending put that team spirit to the test. Toure scored an own goal early on in the game, only for a brilliant pass from Gerrard to set up Sturridge for an equaliser, the eighth game in a row he had found the net in. Liverpool attacked to find a second goal without reward—and were punished on the hour when Kieran Richardson was presented with an easy opportunity.

2-1 to Fulham.

Undeterred, Rodgers' side had built up a belief that they could outscore any opposition by this point and went again, Coutinho equalising this time with a curling shot from 20 yards. Joao Teixeira came on for his debut as Rodgers looked to find a way through for the winner, and the chance they required was presented in the very last minute of the game after Sturridge was crudely chopped down inside the box.

Penalty for Liverpool, penalty for Gerrard...and a last-minute, adrenaline-releasing 3-2 victory was the result.

The FA Cup fifth round against Arsenal provided another opportunity to test themselves against a top side, and despite running Arsenal ragged early on once more, the Reds' clinical edge was missing for once. They suffered a 2-1 defeat at the Emirates and were knocked out as a result, with another Gerrard penalty not enough to get them back into the match this time. Contrasting this defeat to the 2-0 loss in the league at the same ground in November, however, was to compare two very different performances. Liverpool fans and players alike were not unduly disheartened.

It was the Premier League which demanded more focus and attention to continue chasing the Champions League spot which everybody associated with the club wanted, and next in line there was a home game against Swansea City.

Things looked good after 20 minutes when Sturridge and Jordan Henderson had put the Reds two goals up, but a stunning Jonjo Shelvey strike drew applause from the Kop and Skrtel scored yet another own goal moments later, with the scores all level at 2-2 even before the half-hour mark.

Liverpool re-took the lead when Sturridge headed in from close range after a great cross from Suarez, but Skrtel conceded a penalty in the second half which Wilfried Bony scored from. Once again it seemed Liverpool had to show their capacity to outscore the opposition, and Henderson netted his second of the game, his third of the season, to ensure a 4-3 win.

That run of three league wins in a row left the Reds in fourth place at the end of the month, four points off top spot and, importantly, with a six-point gap between themselves and Spurs in fifth.

10. The ever-changing tactics of Brendan Rodgers' Liverpool

By Karl Matchett

It has been said, on rather more than a single occasion, that "Team X are great when things are going well, but they lack a Plan B for those games when the opposition are tough to break down." Often, that Plan B is lazily expected to be a single different style of player; a giant striker, for example.

You look at sides around the Premier League—and further afield—and a recurring theme is that they have a base formation which takes to the field each and every game, regardless of personnel, and little changes aside from the starting names. For some, that's an admirable commitment to stability, to everybody knowing their roles, to a clear strategy in the transfer market. For others, however, it's an absolute hindrance which leads to stagnation—within individual games or over the longer term—to predictability and to resorting to playing in an unfamiliar style late on in matches, as a point or a victory is chased. To entrusting, to a fairly large extent, in luck falling on your side in finding a route to goal.

Brendan Rodgers appears to be in the latter category.

His team has a style of playing: an aggression and an arrogance on the ball, a commitment to attacking football and a demand of controlling play as much as possible, both in terms of spaces on the pitch and of possession itself.

What he does not have, however, is a demand for playing in a single, unyielding tactical deployment. Over the course of his two years at the club so far, Rodgers has altered his tactics at will and as required, suiting his positioning of players to the strengths of his own options and the deficiencies of the opposition. 2013-14 especially has seen the Reds go through the season in three distinct periods: The early 4-2-1-3/4-2-3-1, a middle run of games featuring a flat back three and, for much of the last third of the campaign, a return to the 1-2 midfield shape which has incorporated both a diamond midfield and a true 4-3-3.

There have been anomalies along the way, of course: a misguided and narrow 4-4-2 at home to Aston Villa was one notable variation. There have been others. But, by and large, Rodgers has proven extremely capable of taking on board the tactical lessons from each game—victories and defeats alike—and adding to his collection of knowledge about his players, the roles they can perform in the team and the areas of the pitch in which certain individuals or pairings are vulnerable. Versatility is an important attribute in players, to Rodgers' mind. If a player performs one task particularly well, on the wing, say, can he also do the same from a central role? How about further up the field? These assets and key strengths of players are not just what make them good in a particular position, they are tools to attack any opposition with, from any location.

Early on in the season, Jordan Henderson was deployed on either side of midfield. His strong running, improving tactical awareness and tenacious off-the-ball work made him ideal to support the attack from the channels, but also to retain a semblance of defensive solidity, have numbers tracking back...and then able to break forward once more, at pace, once the ball was back in Red possession.

Henderson also supported the forward, centrally ahead of a midfield double pivot. He also played at wing-back. As a defensive midfielder. And, finally, as perhaps the most important single name on the team-sheet, right in the centre of midfield, where he has dominated, shown great capability in both halves of the pitch and made the entire team flow in the manner Rodgers wants.

The Reds' No. 14 is an extreme example, of course, but he's far from the only one. Those early matches with a double midfield pivot allowed four more offensive players to be constantly in support of a single, central striker, Daniel Sturridge in the first few games. The lineup looked like a 4-2-3-1 on paper, but whether it was a midfield three or a trio of attacking midfielders changed depending on who played that No. 10 role. When it was Iago Aspas, it was certainly a 4-2-3-1, with the wider midfielders not as close to the front two. When Henderson played there, he broke forward from deeper but the wide forwards were just that, forwards, in a 4-2-1-3.

There were problems despite the run of clean sheets early in the season: The players most frequently in the box, Sturridge excepted, were not the best in terms of taking their chances. Goalscoring opportunities were spurned, Luis Suarez remained suspended, a succession of younger players weren't showing themselves as clinical at that point. Further back, Steven Gerrard and Lucas Leiva have their own defensive strengths, but as a pairing they struggled with opposition runners from deep, a painfully recurring theme from 2012-13 and even before that.

So the approach changed. Three at the back gave an additional central body to close out those spaces which were exploited by runners, while the attacking wing-backs—Aly Cissokho, Henderson, Raheem Sterling at one point—were more frequently able to push forward. Liverpool had played with a back three under both Kenny Dalglish and Rafael Benitez, but Rodgers' version differed in attack: he preferred two central forwards and one supporting from an attacking midfield line, whereas previously Reds fans had seen a wide three-man attack in a 3-4-3 or else support from two attacking midfielders for a lone forward. That, of course, has been largely to do with only one decent striker being at the club for a long time.

With Suarez and Sturridge, a 3-5-2 basic shape was seen as the ideal way to pair the deadly attackers together, and try to support from deep.

It certainly worked for a spell and there was a train of thought that, when the likes of Philippe Coutinho and even Jose Enrique returned from injury, those players would have natural roles to slip into within that formation. A back three, at that point, looked as though it may become Liverpool's base system.

Again though, flaws remained. Creativity was reliant on the No. 10 or the two forwards too often, whilst periods of defensive work for Liverpool would see the team sit deep, not break out of their shape and struggle to progress up the field. In games they dominated, they shape worked well and support could get to the front two; where possession was squandered or opponents pressed high in Liverpool's own half, however, it could lead to an isolated attack.

A return to a back four was always likely at some point, but the Reds' end-of-season run of form can be attributed to their midfield shape.

Gerrard's role was changed, he became the deepest player in midfield. By himself, crucially. The triangle was re-flipped, one holding player was back in, with two ahead. Is Gerrard a defensive midfielder? Not a chance. He remains an attacking player, just operating from a far deeper role. That's not to say he doesn't defend; his role is a complex one which he has performed very well in the main. He protects the back four with his lateral movement, a rediscovered willingness to get involved in aerial duels and a habit of clearing second balls as they drop out of defence. But his primary role is that of a creator, a tempo-setter, a constant outlet to recycle, switch and move forward the ball.

With other players in that role—Lucas Leiva, Joe Allen, whoever—they do a similar job in possession but look to lay the ball into midfield. Where Gerrard excels and helps the team far more is that he has a greater passing range, and bucket-loads of additional time and space to make use of that particular skill. He won't only pass the ball 10 yards, but 15, or 30. The next line of midfielders can continue moving, finding space further forward when possible, in the knowledge that Gerrard can find them. That single change has the effect of moving the team further up the field, and by moving Gerrard *out* of the very centre of the team and bringing somebody else *in*, raises the energy and off the ball movement of the side considerably.

With that midfield shape reverting to a 1-2, far better balanced as a result, it left the attack to worry about, and Rodgers' solution has been both exciting and explosive.

The diamond midfield or a 4-3-3 has the same midfield base, but a one-behind-two in attack instead of two-wide-of-one. Even with the same three players usually involved, the flexibility, unpredictability and technical ability of that attack is as good as anything the Premier League has to offer. Next season, the Reds will see if it can match up to Europe's best, too.

SAS became SSS as Sterling, Suarez and Sturridge showed the brilliant movement, tenacity and relentlessness—not to mention a wonderful clinical edge—in the final third which Rodgers had been searching for. It was shown in flashes last season, in more than flashes in the first half of 13-14 (such as against Tottenham or West Brom), but from February onwards it was the hallmark of the Reds' title challenge.

In amongst all that it was easy to overlook Coutinho's altered role, but moving him back into an attacking, but very much *central* midfield position, has had a great impact on the Brazilian. His work-rate has been outstanding in the hungry Liverpool midfield, while the quick transitions of the team see him make the absolute best use of his main skills: carrying the ball into space, acceleration away from opponents and incisive through-passes.

Just one small step further forward to the tip of the diamond, and that last sentence exactly applies to Raheem Sterling, the undoubted star of the second half of Liverpool's season.

Brendan Rodgers has developed a number of players to be better now than they were two years ago, and they're not all necessarily the top players in the team. Sterling's progress alone, though, is worthy of a new contract for the manager. His ideals, his way of playing, his preference of attacking first and then attacking again second...all of it means that Liverpool will remain an exciting side to watch, will win far more games than they lose and *should*, luck and transfers aside, go on to continue challenging at the top end of the league.

Plan B? We've already seen it. And C, and D and others. It's just another of the alterations Rodgers will continue to make as he looks to win each and every game. The continuity, the stability, the feeling of being settled in the side...that all comes from playing the same way. A regular position on the field is only required for a small handful of players, such as the goalkeeper and (hopefully) main defensive partnership. Elsewhere, it's the skills and determination of players, in any and in every role, which help shape the side.

Whatever the opposition brings, whatever methods they employ to stop the Reds, Rodgers and Liverpool can find a way around it. It won't always work. You can't win every match. But far more often than not, as they progress and improve and add to the squad with more options, the team as a whole will manage to overcome these obstacles with different systems but always the same style, substance and swagger.

And that is Brendan Rodgers' version of tactical acumen. A far more preferable one, you'll agree, to others Anfield might have witnessed this season.

11. End of season run-in

By Karl Matchett

March, 2014

Liverpool were unbeaten in the league in 2014 at this point but they faced a tough run of games in March, starting with consecutive away trips to St. Mary's and Old Trafford. Another pair of tests were passed with consummate professionalism and no shortage of attacking talent though; Southampton and Manchester United were both beaten 3-0 on their own turf.

Southampton had chances in the first of those games, especially in the first half, but once Luis Suarez had fired in his first goal since the derby, there was only likely to be one winner, though Simon Mignolet did make a terrific strop from Jay Rodriguez to keep the Reds ahead at the break. The second half saw further assists claimed by the Uruguayan forward as he set up Sterling to score with his first touch after coming on as a sub, before winning a late penalty which Gerrard tucked away.

Old Trafford was not a happy place by the time Liverpool arrived there, sat in seventh place while the Reds were up in third, and it didn't get a whole lot better after the 90 minutes.

Liverpool were far and away the better, more adventurous and more complete team and the 3-0 win was justified, even without the team absolutely going for the kill as they had in previous games. Steven Gerrard scored twice from the penalty spot and hit the post with a third, while Suarez kept his strike rate above a goal per game with a late effort for 3-0.

The Reds were back amongst the goals, and the crazy games, when they took on Cardiff City in their next match.

Manager Brendan Rodgers was at pains to nod at both ends of the pitch after a see-saw 6-3 victory. "We showed our power in the offensive game today. There are areas defensively that we can improve on. The biggest thing from conceding three goals was that we showed the resilience to come back."

He was right on both counts; Liverpool had to come from behind twice in the first half to go in 2-2 at the break, with Suarez and Skrtel notching those goals. Skrtel headed a third before a Sturridge back-heel set up Suarez's own brace, before they swapped roles for the England international to side-foot home the fifth. Cardiff pulled another back in the closing stages, but Suarez wrapped up his hat-trick in stoppage time after running through unchallenged, giving him 28 goals in 25 league games for the season.

At that point, Liverpool went into second place in the league and were on a six-match winning streak; not only was the Champions League looking a likelihood rather than a possibility at that stage, but title talk was unavoidable. With eight games to play, Liverpool were four points off the top with a game in hand, and still had to play both sides above and below them in the league.

First up, though, was a test against relegation candidates Sunderland.

Whether because of the pressure of the title talk, the inevitability of a down-turn in form or because their opponents were in desperate need of points, the Reds found it tough to hit top gear at home against the Black Cats.

A free-kick from Gerrard found the top corner in the first half and a deflected Sturridge strike—his 20th of the league season—did the same after the break, but the comfort of that 2-0 lead disappeared entirely when Ki Sung-Yeung headed in for Sunderland with 15 to play. The Reds did hold on for a seventh successive win, though, closing the gap at the top to a single point.

Spurs visited Anfield at the end of March, but if they were hoping to fare significantly better than in the reverse fixture they were left disappointed.

Younes Kaboul put through his own net within 100 seconds of kick-off and Suarez added a second midway through the half. Coutinho buried a strike from range after Jon Flanagan had shown great skill and movement down the left, before Henderson's free kick beat everybody and crept in at the far post.

Spurs were left to rue another heavy defeat, while the 4-0 win meant Liverpool ended the month with five wins from five games, having scored 18 goals and kept three clean sheets. Unsurprisingly and very much deservedly, Rodgers was named Manager of the Month while Gerrard and Suarez shared the Players' award.

April, 2014

Enter April, and Liverpool were top of the Premier League.

With just six matches to play and the Reds on an eight-game winning streak, there was little point in pretending otherwise: Brendan Rodgers had led Liverpool right into a title challenge, certainly their best season since 2008-09 and with a great possibility of being their finest in the entire Premier League era.

It had to be a case of "same again" though, with a trip to West Ham United next on the agenda. The Reds toiled and struggled at Upton Park, unable to make their usual clever combination plays in the final third.

Suarez won a penalty for hand-ball against James Tomkins which Steven Gerrard dispatched, but a disgraceful non-call by the referee and his assistants meant the teams went in 1-1 at the break. Andy Carroll clearly barged and manhandled Simon Mignolet off a West Ham corner, but with nothing given against the striker, the goalkeeper dropped the ball into the path of Guy Demel who poked home an equaliser.

It was left to Gerrard to score another penalty with 20 minutes left on the clock to win the game for the Reds, after Flanagan was brought down by the Hammers' 'keeper Adrian.

Maybe the biggest game of the season to that point followed, as Manchester City paid their visit to Anfield. Liverpool were top, two points ahead of Chelsea, with City back in third a further two points behind—but with two games in hand. An absolute roller-coaster of a match ensued, with the Reds flying out of the blocks to take a sixth-minute lead through Raheem Sterling. The young forward showed great movement to initially get behind the defence, before composure and technique saw him send Joe Hart and Kompany the wrong way, allowing him to fire home at the near post.

If Anfield wasn't already rocking after that, it certainly was 20 minutes later; Skrtel climbed highest at the near post to divert a Gerrard corner over Hart and into the far side of the goal—2-0 to Liverpool.

Manchester City are noted for their fantastic forward line and impressive mental strength, though, and those qualities came to the fore after the break. David Silva began to dictate play and the Spaniard scored one and created another, the latter going in off Glen Johnson, as the away side came back from two goals down to 2-2 in the space of five minutes.

It's not only City who have resilience and attacking quality, though, as Liverpool had shown throughout the campaign.

The Reds picked themselves up, weathered a bit of a storm and attacked once more—and Philippe Coutinho made Anfield explode with a low, drilled, first-time shot into the bottom corner with 12 minutes to play. With three massive points at stake, Liverpool's defence gave everything to keep City at bay this time, to the extent that Jordan Henderson was over-zealous in the challenge in injury time and found himself red carded.

The celebrations as the final whistle went rivalled anything which happened en-route to Istanbul, Cardiff or Athens during the mid-to-late 2000s, while Steven Gerrard's emotional and inspirational team-talk on the field made sure his team-mates remained focused on the task in hand.

Norwich City were next up and by this time were in a desperate relegation fight.

There was to be no Suarez hat-trick this time, with Raheem Sterling instead taking the limelight for two excellent individual goals—albeit deflected ones—and a sumptuous assist for Suarez's 30th league goal of the campaign.

Norwich twice fought back with goals off lofted balls into the box, but the Reds did enough to record an 11th successive Premier League win, a quite incredible run of form.

The run of wins had to end at some point, of course, but every Kopite would have been hoping it didn't come, of all matches, in the next game, at home to Chelsea.

Liverpool absolutely dominated play from start to finish, with the league's second-place side content to pack their own penalty box and frustrate the home crowd with time-wasting from the very first whistle. While the tactics might have been predictable, Liverpool didn't show enough patience or intelligence in the final third, particularly in the second half, to break Chelsea down.

It might not have mattered; a draw would have kept Liverpool seven points clear of Manchester City, who had two games in hand, while Chelsea would have been five behind with only two to play.

A dreadful, awful piece of luck changed the whole complexion of the game however, and indeed of the Premier League title race, right on the stroke of half-time. Steven Gerrard received the ball inside his own half of the pitch but slipped as he attempted to control and turn; in an instant Demba Ba had whipped the ball past him and the striker ran on to bury the opener past Mignolet.

The side left the pitch to a chorus of support and songs of encouragement from the home crowd, none more so than the captain, but Liverpool couldn't capture their creativity and clinical edge, for so long their best weapon in the title fight, right when they needed it most.

A second goal for Chelsea duly arrived in injury time at the end of the match as the Reds pushed everybody forward, resulting in a 2-0 defeat—Liverpool's first in the league in 2014 and the end of their 11-match winning run.

May, 2014

That loss put the title back in Manchester City's hands; even two wins to end the season would not guarantee the Reds the title, as City's goal difference was superior.

Liverpool travelled to Crystal Palace for their penultimate match of the campaign, knowing they needed to not only win, but win by as many goals as possible to keep their title dreams alive.

Initially that side of things went well. Joe Allen scored his first league goal for Liverpool in the first half, before Sturridge's effort was deflected in by Damian Delaney and Suarez scored a record-equalling 31st Premier League goal for three. With still more than half an hour to play, Liverpool looked comfortable for the three points, but the temptation to go for more goals also lingered.

Was it this, in the end, which saw the collapse which ensued? It didn't seem to be. Instead it was more an attitude of "match over" which saw defensive deficiencies once again rear their head, with Liverpool throwing two points away in dramatic style in the final 12 minutes of the game. Delaney found the top corner via a deflection from 25 yards, before substitute Dwight Gayle scored twice in seven minutes.

Poor decision-making, a lack of leadership or a simple absence of composure: whatever the reasons, Liverpool's league title hopes had disintegrated after the last two games, as they left Selhurt Park with a 3-3 draw and a single point.

And so to the final day of the season.

Manchester City had gone top and played at home on the last day, leaving Liverpool in the almost-certain knowledge that they faced Newcastle United for pride, for the fans, but ultimately for second place. Having come into the season hoping for a top-four finish, that there was an air of resigned acceptance about Anfield for the match which spoke volumes of just how far the team had come, something the supporters acknowledged after the game.

As an event, the match was frustrating in the first half—poor control, lacking movement, not much ingenuity—and the Reds went in at the break 1-0 down, with another Skrtel own goal doing the damage.

In it's own way, though, the game was a microcosm of Liverpool's improvements during 2013-14: they showed great mentality and resilience, there was an attacking threat, set pieces were made great use of and home advantage remained a force at the club's disposal. Two Gerrard free-kicks were finished off at the far post by Daniel Agger and Daniel Sturridge, giving the Reds a winning end to a remarkable season and guaranteeing a second-place finish above Chelsea and Arsenal, just two points behind City.

The end-of-season lap of the pitch by the players brought great acclaim from the supporters who knew their heroes had given them more than they'd had a right to hope for over the past 10 months, while the last word of the year, fittingly, should go to the man who has masterminded what is surely only the beginning of Liverpool's journey back toward the top of English football.

"The style will only be enhanced and improved. We will definitely strengthen and we will be better next season. There will be no fear; we'll come back mentally, tactically and technically ready."

With Champions League football back at Anfield for 2014-15 and their highest league position in five years achieved, Liverpool fans have every reason to look forward with excitement, trust and belief in what Brendan Rodgers and his Liverpool players might go on to achieve next season.

12. Best and worst of 2013-14

By Henry Jackson

Best Player: Luis Suarez

27-year-old forward Luis Suarez was undeniably the standout performer all season long, not just at Liverpool but also in the Premier League. 31 goals in 37 matches in all competitions is a phenomenal achievement, particularly when the fact he doesn't take the teams penalties is taken into account. Whether it was the four goals against Norwich, the sublime free-kick away to Everton or multiple other pieces of genius, Suarez was utterly untouchable and a case could certainly be made for him being labelled the world's best player in 2013-14. His skill, creativity and sheer work-rate for the good of the team are unrivalled and if he stays at Liverpool for the foreseeable future there is no reason why he can't rival Kenny Dalglish and Steven Gerrard as one of the club's greatest ever players.

Best Young Player: Raheem Sterling

Jordan Henderson certainly pushed Raheem Sterling close, but the 19-year-old's journey from first-team bench-warmer to key player this season has been sensational. His electrifying pace, quick feet and excellent end product have caused the country's best defences no end of problems since the beginning of December. Sterling simply got better and better as the season progressed from that point. 10 goals in 35 appearances in all competitions are highly impressive statistics for a player so young still, and the fact he scored against the likes of Arsenal and Manchester City shows he doesn't shy away in the big games. Liverpool have an exceptional talent on their hands, another who could go on to become a future Reds legend if he stays grounded and continues to improve.

Worst Player: Victor Moses

Although Victor Moses may have had a little more effect on games than some other poor performers, the general attitude that the on-loan Chelsea winger showed was simply not good enough at times. Too often he failed to track back and do his defensive work, while at the other end his final ball, decision making and off the ball movement left a lot to be desired. Just when he had the chance to make himself a hero and score the winner at Crystal Palace in stoppage time, he fluffed his lines further. Two goals in 22 appearances, and no assists, does not represent a good return for an attacking player.

Best Goal: Luis Suarez vs. Norwich City (first goal)

Suarez's first goal in the 5-1 thrashing over Norwich just gets the nod over his equally brilliant third effort out of four on the night. The Uruguayan's dipping volley from all of 40 yards in front of the Kop was truly sensational, perfectly summing up the genius of El Pistolero. He is, without doubt, John Ruddy's lasting nemesis.

Best Game: Liverpool 5-1 Arsenal

In what was arguably the Reds' greatest league display since dispatching of Nottingham Forest 5-0 in 1988, Brendan Rodgers' side annihilated Arsenal on an unforgettable day at Anfield in February 2014. Martin Skrtel scored within the opening two minutes and got his second soon after with a towering header. Raheem Sterling added a third after a typically free-flowing move, before Daniel Sturridge added a fourth with just 20 minutes on the clock—it was absolutely breathless. Sterling prodded in a fifth at the second attempt after the break and, as Liverpool took their foot of the gas, Mikel Arteta's penalty proved a minor consolation for the Gunners. Hugely impressive drubbings of Everton, Spurs (twice) and Manchester United also stand out in a season of memorable beatings handed out to rivals.

Worst Game: Crystal Palace 3-3 Liverpool

A night that appeared to be going so smoothly turned into a nightmare in Liverpool's penultimate game of the season. A win was needed to keep the pressure on Manchester City in the title race, and goals from Joe Allen, a deflected Daniel Sturridge strike (later credited as a Damien Delaney own goal) and Luis Suarez looked to have sealed all three points. With the Reds going gung-ho in order to narrow the goal difference between themselves and City, they capitulated defensively in the final 11 minutes. Delaney's deflected effort got Palace back into it, and two goals from substitute Dwight Gayle stunned the visitors. It realistically signalled the end of the Reds' title dreams. The 3-1 defeat away to Hull is worthy of a mention too as the worst team performance of the campaign.

Most Important Victory: Fulham 2-3 Liverpool

With fourth place still the priority this was a huge win, with Spurs breathing down Liverpool's necks in fifth. Kolo Toure's disastrous own goal was cancelled out by Sturridge, but Kieran Richardson put Fulham back ahead in the second-half. Philippe Coutinho's strike made it 2-2 with 18 minutes remaining and, just as it looked as if the game was drifting towards a draw, Steven Gerrard converted a last-gasp penalty to send the away fans into raptures. It was a key moment in Liverpool's season; things may have panned out very differently had they drawn.

Best Signing: Mamadou Sakho

It's probably fair to say that none of the signings in 2013-14 were an enormous success, but Mamadou Sakho certainly impressed at times. The 24-year-old France international fitted in nicely, displaying a calm head, great composure on the ball and good pace. Injuries hampered him, however, and he struggled to put together a long run in the side at any point. He has all the attributes to become a top-class defender at Anfield in the future.

Worst Signing: Iago Aspas

The Spaniard showed some promising form in pre-season following his move from Celta Vigo, but was a huge disappointment. The 26-year-old never got used to the physical style of the Premier League, failing to score in his 14 appearances, with his only goal coming in the FA Cup win over Oldham in January. If anyone was still trying to stick up for Apsas prior to the loss to Chelsea in May, his late cameo in that match would have completely swayed their opinions.

13. Squad profiles

By Henry Jackson and Jack Lusby

Simon Mignolet, goalkeeper

Life as a Liverpool player could not have started any better for Simon Mignolet, as his late penalty save against Stoke on the opening day ensured the Reds won 1-0.

Clean sheets against Aston Villa and Manchester United followed, meaning the Belgian didn't concede in the league until mid-September. His fine form continued until December—he was outstanding in the 3-3 draw with Everton—but errors began creeping in at key times.

Mistakes against Manchester City and Chelsea played a big part in Liverpool losing both games 2-1, while further shaky displays against Stoke City and Aston Villa at home had many questioning the former Sunderland stopper.

Despite the odd error now and then, Mignolet has largely impressed in his first season as the new Liverpool goalkeeper. A terrific shot-stopper, the 26-year-old needs to improve on the aerial aspect of his game if he is to match or surpass his predecessor Pepe Reina.

2013-14 mark (out of 10): 7

Squad Status Next Season: First XI

Brad Jones, goalkeeper

Australian shot-stopper Brad Jones continued his tenure as Liverpool's backup goalkeeper this season and—with the signing of Simon Mignolet from Sunderland in the summer proving a largely astute one—failed to make an appearance in the Premier League in 2013-14.

Jones' only appearances came in the Reds' ill-fated FA Cup run, against Oldham Athletic, AFC Bournemouth and Arsenal. The 32-year-old performed admirably in these fixtures, keeping clean sheets against both Oldham and Bournemouth, whilst he can blame a disjointed defence for the pair of goals conceded at the Emirates as Liverpool's cup run came to an end.

Unfortunately for Jones, his qualities—even as a backup goalkeeper—don't suit the demands of either an extended Premier League or Champions League campaign, and as such may find his time at Anfield coming to an end sooner rather than later.

Mark: 6

Squad Status Next Season: Sold, or at least replaced as No. 2

Glen Johnson, right-back

The 29-year-old had an inconsistent season, showing signs of excellence one minute but then producing some hugely below-par performances the next.

After looking good in the opening three league matches, an ankle injury saw Johnson ruled out for six weeks. When he returned he was very poor and looked close to disinterested at times. It was clear the England international was not 100 per cent fit, and he was ruled out for a further month in January after more trouble with his ankle and groin.

Since overcoming those issues the right-back initially showed improved form, playing with more confidence and attacking thrust than previously. The defensive weaknesses still remain, however, and his end-of-season form was amongst the poorest of the players who featured for the Reds. With just one year left on his contract there is every chance the former West Ham man could leave Anfield in the summer after five solid years at the club.

Mark: 5

Squad Status Next Season: Sold

Martin Kelly, right-back

Returning following the summer break sporting an Alberto Aquilani-esque hairstyle, local-lad Kelly's barbershop exploits this season have somewhat matched his former team-mate's position within the Liverpool squad, as he found himself outcast in quite the same way the Italian playmaker did in Brendan Rodgers' first season in charge.

The 24-year-old made five Premier League appearances this season, all from the substitute's bench, with a further three appearances in cup competitions, against Oldham Athletic and AFC Bournemouth in the FA Cup and in the Reds' 1-0 Capital One Cup loss away to Manchester United. In another season stunted by injury—the defender began the season in rehabilitation following ACL damage—Kelly finds his options diminishing. Following the drastic progress of another Liverpool academy graduate, Jon Flanagan, at full-back, Kelly's opportunity to break through into the first-team on a regular basis seems bleaker by the month. Brendan Rodgers hinted he'll get his chance next season, but that seems likely to only be as a cover player.

Mark: 5

Squad Status Next Season: Squad player at best

Jon Flanagan, full-back

Prior to the start of the season, Jon Flanagan was a squad player at best who many felt would never make it as a Liverpool player. How wrong they were.

The 21-year-old was thrown into action against Arsenal in November, but on a disappointing evening for the Reds Flanagan was one of the few positives. From that point on, he never looked back. His performance in the Merseyside derby soon after was fantastic and Steven Gerrard claimed that the entire squad applauded the youngster when he returned to the changing room after the match.

Flanagan's own personal highlight of the season came in the 5-0 win at Tottenham, when he fired home his first ever goal for his boyhood team. The reaction of his team-mates perfectly highlighted what a popular member of the squad he now is. Passionate, robust in the tackle and underrated going forward, Flanagan has had a terrific season.

Mark: 8

Squad Status Next Season: Rotation

Martin Skrtel, centre-back

In a season of continued defensive insecurity, wherein which Liverpool conceded 50 goals and often had to rely on their majestic forward line to outscore their opponents, the resurgence of Slovakian centre-back Martin Skrtel can be considered a true highlight.

Having only made 25 Premier League appearances for the Reds in the 2012/13 season—losing his place at the heart of the defence to Jamie Carragher over the second half of the campaign—it was much-speculated that Skrtel would leave the club in the summer, with Rafa Benitez's Napoli the likely destination. However, to his credit, Skrtel buckled down and ended up keeping his place in Rodgers' side on defensive merit.

One of the biggest criticisms of Skrtel over the years is that he lacks composure on the ball, but this season he has moulded his game and become one of the side's most accurate passers. Often opting to keep things simple, his new-found approach suits the style of Rodgers' Liverpool. However, he has also been seen rampaging forward in swashbuckling style, aiding quick transitions in play and providing an unexpected extra body moving forward at times. This is not to say the 29-year-old has abandoned his uncompromising defensive approach; in terms of defensive actions—making clearances, interceptions and making vital blocks—he is the Premier League's most prolific defender.

Arguably the most outstanding contribution from the Slovakian this season has been in terms of goalscoring. Previously renowned only for his uncanny ability to land the ball in his own net, Skrtel scored seven Premier League goals this season. An early double in the impressive 5-1 victory over Arsenal at Anfield was followed by another brace in the Reds' 6-3 away win at Cardiff City. Having an additional number of players taking the pressure off Luis Suarez and Daniel Sturridge in terms of goalscoring has been important in Liverpool's title challenge this season, and Skrtel has been one of those to contribute most. Of course, he also diminished that impact somewhat by netting own goals against Hull City, West Ham, Swansea City and Newcastle United.

Doubts still remain over Skrtel's long-term future at Liverpool, and the Reds' leaky defence can definitely be improved upon, but the centre-back's contribution this season will have no doubt endeared him to Rodgers, making it will likely that he will remain at Anfield beyond this summer.

Mark: 8

Squad Status Next Season: Rotation

Mamadou Sakho, centre-back

Aggressive French centre-back Sakho moved to Liverpool from Ligue 1 champions Paris Saint-Germain in the summer for a reported fee of around £18 million, and was described by Reds' managing director Ian Ayre as a "marquee signing". The 24-year-old duly arrived at Anfield with a high level of prestige, having captained the French side at the young age of 17 years old.

Arguably signed as the long-term replacement for a waning Daniel Agger, Sakho has performed at a consistently high level for Liverpool in 2013/14. However, the French international has struggled at times with injury, and as such has failed to tie down a regular first-team place as of yet; the Reds' No. 17 made 18 league appearances this season, scoring one goal. Next term, the burgeoning centre-back will look to make the position on the left side of defence his own—be it alongside Martin Skrtel, Tiago Ilori or a new signing—and can consider himself very much a key player for the future.

Mark: 7

Squad Status Next Season: Regular first XI starter

Daniel Agger, centre-back

Daniel Agger's season started on a high note, with Rodgers making the 29-year-old Liverpool's vice-captain following the retirement of Jamie Carragher. Although he started as a regular, assisting Daniel Sturridge in the Reds' 1-0 win over Manchester United in September, as the season progressed both injuries and form hampered the Dane.

While he was as elegant on the ball as ever, some of his defensive work did leave a lot to be desired, with his competence at defending set pieces a particular weakness. Agger scored twice during the campaign: at home to Hull City, and then on the final day of the season against Newcastle United. Mamadou Sakho now looks clearly first choice ahead of Agger and, after eight years of service, the end seems nigh for the classy centre-back.

Mark: 6

Squad Status Next Season: Sold

Kolo Toure, centre-back

Former Manchester City defender Kolo Toure saw his Liverpool career start promisingly, but it soon became progressively worse. The 33-year-old was solid up until the 2-0 defeat against Arsenal in November, in which he was poor, and from that point on he was a fringe player at best.

His lowest point came in February at West Brom. With Liverpool winning 1-0, his disastrous pass went straight to Victor Anichebe, who equalised for the hosts, costing the Reds two vital points. Two games later, his calamitous own goal against Fulham almost cost Liverpool again, but fortunately for Toure the attacking power of the team won through on that occasion.

At times he's appeared to be an accident waiting to happen; for all of his vast experience there were times when he played like a nervy debutant. Even so, key contributions such as his lofted pass for Daniel Sturridge's lobbed goal against Everton should be remembered. Off the field, his huge character and winning mentality were certainly plus points, but barring a decent start, Toure has struggled to be a success.

Mark: 5

Squad Status Next Season: Sold

Jose Enrique, left-back

Spanish left-back Enrique started the season with Liverpool in good form, contributing to an admirable run of three consecutive clean sheets—three 1-0 victories—in the side's first three league games. However, three further starts and two more substitute appearances aside, the rest of the 28-year-old's season can be considered a write-off.

In those eight league appearances, Enrique helped ensure the Reds conceded only five goals and contributed with two assists at the other end of the pitch; however, persistent injury problems have curtailed any advance on this impressive return. The muscular full-back underwent surgery on an ongoing knee problem in November and hasn't featured since. Despite the development of Jon Flanagan at left-back this season, it is likely that Rodgers will look to reinforce that position in the summer and, if Enrique's problems continue—despite a valiant contribution when fit—the Spaniard will have to settle for a squad role at best next season.

Mark: 6

Squad Status Next Season: Squad player or sold

Aly Cissokho, left-back

Liverpool's on-loan French left-back Aly Cissokho joined on a season-long deal from Valencia to little fanfare in August and has done little to light up Anfield since. Such have been his poor performances that many have quipped that he must have the best agent in the game.

Making his Premier League debut as a late substitute for Iago Aspas against Aston Villa, Cissokho's first contribution to the Reds' cause was a wayward throw-in and the rest of his Liverpool career has followed suit. Injury hampered any form of progress and, whilst his form did improve after the new year and he showed better defensive aptitude, he has remained understandably on the sideline for much of the season. Absence has made the heart grow fonder, however, and Cissokho has become something of a cult figure on Merseyside—a hugely deflected long-range goal against Stoke City will long remain a highlight of the season. Nevertheless, the Frenchman has little chance of a renewed deal this summer.

Mark: 5

Squad Status Next Season: Loan ended and a return to his parent club.

Lucas Leiva, central midfield

The 2013-14 season was a hugely frustrating one for the Brazilian, with injuries once again proving disastrous for the 27-year-old's progress in a Red shirt. Having performed well on occasion in the opening half of the season, bringing a typically calm and assured presence to the midfield, Lucas picked up a knee injury in the draw with Aston Villa in January. He missed two months after that, and failed to cement his place as a regular from that point on. Even beforehand, Liverpool's midfield shape hadn't looked quite right and a change in tactic meant his impact on the team was limited.

The odd cameo here and there have been the Brazilian's limit of late and, when he did play, he looked like a player with whom injuries have taken their toll on. It's such a shame that the midfielder is not the influence he was a few years ago, but with Rodgers clearly looking to strengthen his squad this summer, Lucas' Liverpool future doesn't look as secure as it once did.

Mark: 6

Squad Status Next Season: Squad player or sold

Steven Gerrard, central midfield

Steven Gerrard may forever blame himself for Liverpool not winning the 2013-14 Premier League because of one mistake, but without him the Reds would never have got close in the first place. The 33-year-old skipper had a good, if not great, first few months of the season, producing some influential performances and scoring successive penalties against Crystal Palace and Newcastle—the latter being the 100th Premier League goal of his outstanding career.

When he produced a disappointing display in the 2-0 loss at Arsenal in November, many felt he was a shadow of his former self and that his days were numbered, a feeling which intensified after the captain picked up a hamstring injury against West Ham and the team performed admirably without him.

Since his return in January, however, the captain has been magnificent. Brendan Rodgers altered his role in the side, turning him into a deep-lying playmaker in the mould of Andrea Pirlo, and it proved to be an absolute masterstroke. He inspired his side to a 4-0 win over Everton, scoring the opener, before his late spot-kick at Fulham earned Liverpool three huge points. Goals from penalties and terrific set piece delivery all season long meant Gerrard was a regular contributor to the attack, despite his deeper position on the field.

His disastrous slip against Chelsea proved to be a big moment in the title race, but the level of brilliance shown by Liverpool's evergreen skipper throughout the season, particularly from January onwards, makes it impossible to blame him one iota—after all, that result came after a great winning run in which

Gerrard fully played his part, while needless points were dropped earlier in the season. Gerrard ended the campaign with 13 goals and 13 assists in 34 Premier League matches.

Mark: 9

Squad Status Next Season: Regular first XI starter

Joe Allen, central midfield

Welsh midfielder Allen can consider himself one of the Reds' most developed talents this season, as he has adapted his role in the middle of the park to suit Brendan Rodgers' system more adeptly. Dubbed the 'Welsh Xavi' upon his arrival, Allen has now tailored his game into a more high-octane pressing game, and is one of Liverpool's most effective defensive players in 2013/14. Sidelined for an extended period due to much-needed shoulder surgery on a long-term issue, Allen initially struggled to gain a foothold on the Liverpool team this term but has now established himself an important figure for Rodgers' side.

Next season, Allen will look to continue his progress and, following his first Premier League goal for Liverpool against Crystal Palace in the penultimate game of the season, will likely aim to follow Jordan Henderson's example and add more goals and assists to his game. An important figure for years to come.

Mark: 8

Squad Status Next Season: Rotation as a midfield starter

Jordan Henderson, central midfield

For all the brilliance of Suarez, Gerrard and Sturridge, Jordan Henderson was the driving force and underrated presence behind Liverpool's success this season. The effort he put in to becoming a better footballer since his dark early days at the club has been truly admirable. The 23-year-old nearly joined Fulham last summer, with Rodgers unconvinced he was good enough for Liverpool, but the fact he started every Premier League game—barring when suspended—shows exactly what his manager thinks of him now. Earlier in 2013-14 he played in various positions, from left midfield to right wing-back, before cementing a central midfield position later on.

His first goal of the season was a terrific solo effort against Notts County in the Capital One Cup, and the drive, pace and confidence he showed epitomised what was to come for the rest of the campaign. Henderson was outstanding in the 5-0 win over Spurs in December, earning the Man of the Match award and stepping up to the plate with Gerrard out injured. His ability to help win the ball back and quickly surge forward was crucial in wins over the likes of Arsenal and Fulham, to name but two games.

One of the England international's most influential performances came in the 4-3 victory over Swansea in February. His sublime curled effort put his side 2-0 up and then, with the Swans having battled back to 3-3, he scored at the second attempt in front of the Kop to net the crucial winner.

Henderson's suspension following his sending off against

Manchester City in April hurt his side badly, with his importance perhaps only properly highlighted when the dynamic box-to-box man wasn't in the team. Without him, the midfield lacks real endeavour and energy at times, with the ability to press relentlessly and make powerful runs into the final third extremely noticeable.

Henderson is now a very important player at the club, and he deserves every bit of praise he receives.

Mark: 9

Squad Status Next Season: Regular first XI starter

Philippe Coutinho, attacking midfield

Brazilian playmaker Coutinho was an immediate success on Merseyside following his arrival at the club in January of 2013, with his eye for a pass and mesmeric ball control making the youngster a fan favourite.

A young player who teams would soon start paying more attention to, though, it was almost inevitable that 'second season syndrome' would kick in at some point.

Struggling at times to regain the consistent form that made him such a star in the first half of 2013, it seemed that 21-year-old's position in the Liverpool first team was no longer untouchable. However, Coutinho ended the season with a newly-discovered tenacity, and this was crucial in the Reds' 3-2 victory over Manchester City during their title charge as well as other big victories earlier on in the year. Playing more as a third central midfielder over the second half of the season seemed to suit his game more, allowing Coutinho to break forward into space, and his link-up play and passes from deep benefited as a result.

Many forget that the Brazilian is only 21 years old, and as such has plenty of years ahead of him to continue his progress. Next season, Coutinho will no doubt remain a key figure for Rodgers, and the Anfield faithful will surely see him develop further under his manager's stewardship.

Mark: 8

Squad Status Next Season: Regular first XI starter

Raheem Sterling, attacking midfield

The 2013-14 season has played out as a story of redemption for Liverpool's prodigious winger, with the plaudits Raheem Sterling has earned at this season's end marking an incredible period of development over the past 18 months.

Following an impressive season under Rodgers in 2012-13, the Jamaican-born midfielder began this season at somewhat of a canter; largely having to content himself with substitute appearances, the 19-year-old's only start before December came in the Reds' 3-1 demolition of Ian Holloway's Crystal Palace at Anfield in October. A loan move for the youngster was touted, with Brighton a rumoured destination, and few would have argued against such a deal—however, this was quickly refuted by

Rodgers and Sterling has become a mainstay in the Liverpool first team ever since.

Since the beginning of December, Sterling has started all but three of Liverpool's league games, and his improvement over this period has been remarkable. The midfielder has proved himself to be a hugely versatile option for Rodgers, as the Northern Irishman has tailored his formation to suit the task at hand. Initially considered a straight-forward winger, Sterling has featured on both the right and left flanks of the attack, as well as playing at the tip of a midfield diamond; crucially, in each of these positions the youngster has maintained a high level of consistency. Another hugely developed aspect of Sterling's game is his defensive work. In Rodgers' pressing system the work-rate of midfielders such as Sterling is integral and, despite being the smallest player in the squad, the 19-year-old has proven to be one of the strongest defensively.

With goals against Arsenal and Manchester City further underlining his confidence in big-game situations, Sterling can already consider himself a key option for Rodgers' Liverpool side. Next season, Liverpool fans can no doubt look forward to further development as Sterling continues to prove himself as the most talented young player in the Premier League.

Mark: 9

Squad Status Next Season: Regular first XI starter

Luis Alberto, attacking midfield

When Liverpool signed Luis Alberto from Sevilla last summer, many felt the Spaniard could possibly become a first-team regular in 2013-14. He has had a tough first year in England, however, both on and off the pitch. He made his Reds debut against Notts County in the Capital One Cup, but was restricted to brief cameo roles until the turn of the year. Although silky on the ball and possessing typical Spanish elegance in possession, barring an assist for Luis Suarez in the 5-0 win over Spurs he lacked influence.

He made his first start since August against Oldham in the FA Cup in January, but was replaced at half-time. After that, his only appearance came as a 78th-minute substitute in the win over Everton. The 21-year-old has struggled to adapt to the Premier League, while a drink-driving ban certainly hasn't helped matters. It's too soon to properly judge Alberto, but he must improve next season.

Mark: 4

Squad Status Next Season: Squad player or loaned out

Victor Moses, forward

For all the great success stories at Liverpool this season, it's fair to say that Rodgers' decision to sign Victor Moses on a season-long loan from Chelsea was a failure. The Nigerian international actually started his Reds career well, scoring on his debut against

Swansea City with an excellent solo effort. He brought pace out wide that Liverpool have so often lacked, but he struggled to nail down a place for the rest of the campaign.

The 23-year-old often disappointed when he was given the chance to shine from the substitutes bench, lacking a willingness to fight for the cause or get himself involved, and a goal at Bournemouth in FA Cup was the only other thing of real note he produced at the club. There is no doubting that he will be shipped back to Chelsea this summer and he is not a player who will be remembered particularly fondly by supporters. Especially for *that* miss against Crystal Palace.

Mark: 4

Squad Status Next Season: Loan ended and a return to his parent club

Iago Aspas, forward

A hugely impressive pre-season belies the impact Spanish striker Iago Aspas has made for Liverpool this season. A questionable signing from the start, the 26-year-old has been a constant disappointment for the Reds in 2013-14. Signed from Celta Vigo for £7 million in the summer, Aspas boasted a healthy return of 12 goals in 34 league appearances as he helped his side avoid relegation from La Liga. Presumably brought in to relieve some of the pressure from Liverpool's primary strike partnership of Suarez and Sturridge, the forward has scored just one goal this season, against Oldham Athletic in the FA Cup.

His dismally-struck corner in the closing stages of Liverpool's 2-0 defeat to Chelsea at Anfield symbolically sealed Aspas' fate for many Reds fans and, with Rodgers likely to bolster his attacking ranks this summer—aided by the likely return of Fabio Borini—few could argue that the Spaniard warrants a long-term role.

Mark: 4

Squad Status Next Season: Sold

Daniel Sturridge, forward

A successful first five months at Liverpool following his transfer in January 2012 was followed up by a tremendously successful first full season in 2013-14, as Daniel Sturridge continued his development under Brendan Rodgers.

His partnership with Luis Suarez has gone from great to outstanding and the pair's goals aided Liverpool's title aspirations immeasurably. In 29 league appearances this season, Sturridge scored 21 goals—that he didn't finish as he club's top scorer is a testament to the phenomenal season of his strike partner—and will look to continue this form for years to come. What is Chelsea's loss is Liverpool's gain; next season Sturridge will continue his ascent toward world-class status, as Rodgers has judged his potential ceiling, and will once more play a key role as the Reds look to challenge for honours in the Premier League and the Champions League.

Mark: 9

Squad Status Next Season: Regular first XI starter

Luis Suarez, forward

El Pistolero's season can be summed up in one word: Goals.

Suarez scored twice in his first league game back from suspension, against Sunderland, and he found the net again in his next match against Crystal Palace. A hat-trick against West Brom, two more against Fulham, a derby goal at Goodison Park...Suarez was on top of his game at the beginning of the season and his impact on the Liverpool team showed it.

His display in the 5-1 victory over Norwich in December was arguably the finest individual performance of the season, as he scored four of the Reds' five goals, including two Goal of the Season contenders. It was 19 league goals for the season before the turn of the year, and he'd missed the first five matches.

Despite a couple of brief dips in terms of his goal return, Suarez ended the season with 31 in 37 games and went on to win both the PFA Player of the Year and FWA Footballer of the Year awards, as well as sharing the European Golden Shoe award with Cristiano Ronaldo for the top scorer in Europe.

Suarez is, quite simply, the finest current footballer in the Premier League.

Mark: 10

Squad Status Next Season: Regular first XI starter

14. Brendan Rodgers in Profile

By Tom McMahon

Name: Brendan Rodgers
Date of Birth: 26/01/1973
Place of Birth: Carnlough, Northern Ireland
Education: Ballymena, Northern Ireland
Playing Position: Left-back, left Midfielder

Playing Career:

1985 – 1989:	Star United/Ballymena United
1990 – 1993:	Reading
1993–1994:	Newport FC
1994-95:	Whitney Town
1995-96:	Newbury Town

International Career:

1988	Northern Ireland Schools

Managerial Career:

1993-2004:	Reading (Youth Coach)
2004-2008:	Chelsea (Youth Coach)
2008-2009:	Watford
2009:	Reading
2010-2012:	Swansea City
2012:	Liverpool

Honours: Championship play-offs: 2010-11

Biography

Brendan Rodgers may be at the helm at one of world football's largest and most decorated institutions, but the Ulsterman—not born with the silver spoon in his mouth—owes much to his success to his natural charisma, hard graft and a passion for developing technical footballers.

Born to parents Malanchy and Christina Rodgers, Brendan was raised in the humble seaside village of Carnlough, County Antrim in Northern Ireland. Despite Rodgers being regarded as a great sporting all-rounder in his childhood, Brendan did not play competitive football until the age of 13. With Carnlough being too small to have a youth football side, Rodgers' first exposure to the beautiful game was not until he attended St Patrick's college in the neighbouring town of Ballymena.

Recommended by a childhood friend, Rodgers joined local side Star United; regarded as an energetic and talented midfielder, noted for his confidence and dedication both on and off the pitch, Rodgers went on to excel for Ballymena United and represented Northern Ireland at schoolboy level. The Ulsterman then went on trial at a variety of clubs at England—including Manchester United—but chose to settle at Reading FC due to the town's rich Irish community and the strong impression left by then-manager Ian Branfoot.

Despite signing for Reading, Rodgers never played for or even trained with the first team squad. His progress was hindered by a genetic knee condition which also prevented two of his brothers having professional careers. With Rodgers' brittle knees preventing him from playing at the level he desired, Brendan made the bold decision, at the tender age of 20, to retire from professional football in order to focus on coaching.

Youth Coaching

Unlike some professional footballers-turned-coaches, Rodgers faced a difficult route to the top-level of management. Having to work at a nearby John Lewis warehouse to financially support his young family, Rodgers worked part-time in the evenings to coach Reading's Under 5's and to complete his coaching badges. He eventually went full-time and progressed through the youth coaching age groups up to the Under-18s, augmenting his footballing education by studying football philosophies and tactics in Holland and Spain. Rodgers was eventually promoted to academy manager for the Reading youth team.

With a football philosophy sculpted around the 4-3-3 formation, Brendan Rodgers was earning plaudits and connections through his attractive style of play. When Chelsea had vacancies to fill in their youth coaching facility, Jose Mourinho approached Brendan in 2004 after a recommendation from assistant manager Steve Clarke. Upon interviewing him, Mourinho instantly built a rapport with Rodgers, with the Chelsea manager impressed by his tactical nous and shared belief in organisation and hard work.

Shortly after, Brendan Rodgers' fledging Reading side trounced Chelsea's youth team on their own training pitch, paving the way for Brendan Rodgers to become Head Youth Coach at Chelsea's prestigious academy. Brendan was promoted to reserve team manager two years later, which he remained under Mourinho's successors Avram Grant and Luiz Felipe Scolari.

Managerial Career

With Rodgers' flourishing reputation within football circles, the Watford hierarchy recognised him as the model of candidate they were after: a young, up-and-coming manager with fresh philosophies of play. The club soon appointed Rodgers in November 2008, taking over duties from caretaker-manager Malky Mackay, who Brendan kept on as a coach.

Rodgers received a baptism of fire upon his first taste as first-team manager, only winning two of his first ten games with the Hornets. Rodgers tried to make his mark on the team, only to find the club to be flirting with relegation in January. Brendan's patience soon paid off, steering the club to safety by winning eight of the last 16 fixtures and finishing a respectable 13th place in the league.

Reading FC

After Reading failed to secure promotion back to the top-flight, manager Steve Coppell handed in his resignation. Rodgers, having spent most of his life at the club, instantly became favourite to replace Coppell as manager. With Rodgers' previous associations with the club, he felt that he would have been allowed the time and patience to rebuild the squad and achieve success in the long-term. With the club close to his heart, the Ulsterman felt that it was his duty to return Reading to the Premier League and was appointed manager in early June, 2009.

Unfortunately for Rodgers, the fairy-tale appointment was short-lived. He struggled to implement the seismic change which the club required, regularly playing youth players and trying to change the on-field mantra from robust to expansive. This radical transformation resulted in The Royals only picking up two home wins in 12 home games, hovering just one place above the relegation zone. One day after celebrating at the club's Christmas party, Rodgers was sacked as Reading manager—the only dismissal in his career to date.

Rodgers faced six months out of the game, a period in which he reflected on his short career so far. After losing his mother to a sudden heart-attack shortly after his dismissal, Rodgers struggled to come to terms with losing two of the biggest voids in his life. For a time he struggled to secure a position at a new club, with many teams—including League One outfits—refusing to even invite him to interview. Rodgers felt, for the first time in his career, outside the football vacuum. Contemplating a return to coaching under Roberto Mancini's Manchester City, Rodgers thought his career as manager was over before it had even started.

Swansea City

One fateful day, Rodgers was with his children, Anton and Mischa, at a fast-food restaurant when he received a phone-call from Swansea City declaring their interest. The following week Rodgers signed a one-year rolling contract and was unveiled as the Swans' new manager in mid-July 2010, giving him another chance to revive his career in the Football League Championship.

It was at Swansea City in which Brendan Rodgers truly made his stamp on the football world. Rodgers began to look at management more clinically, no longer giving extra chances to players who did not take to his ideas or improve the team performance. A refreshed and revitalised Rodgers steered the club to a third-placed finish, with the strongest home form and defence in the league. After knocking out promotion favourites Nottingham Forest to secure Swansea's place in the play-off final, Rodgers' Swansea were just one victory away from Premier League football. Their opponent, of course, Rodgers knew all too well.

On May 30, 2011, Swansea faced their Wembley adversaries Reading FC—the team which sacked Brendan Rodgers just 17 months previously.

Scott Sinclair, a player which Rodgers brought in on loan from former club Chelsea, scored a hat-trick in a 4-2 win, ensuring that the Swans would be the first Welsh side to ever play in the English top-flight. Despite securing promotion to the Premier League in poetic fashion, Rodgers showed his class by consoling the Royals' manager Brian McDermott and Reading chairman

John Madejski before receiving the trophy. In just one season, Brendan Rodgers has turned around his career in emphatic fashion.

Despite promotion being the pinnacle of Rodgers' career at that point, he knew he faced an uphill battle keeping Swansea in the Premier League. One publication claimed that there was greater chance of seeing Elvis alive than seeing Swansea survive relegation the following season, but Rodgers was confident that his improving side could cause some surprises.

Throughout the 2011-12 campaign, Rodgers' team received plaudits for their attractive and expansive passing style, infamously being dubbed 'Swanselona' by pundits and fans. Notably, in November, Rodgers' Swansea side out-passed and dominated a Liverpool side at Anfield, receiving a standing ovation from The Kop for their emphatic display. Rodgers later told the players to make a note of that moment in their diaries, viewing the moment as a significant sign of progress.

Rodgers' Swansea continued to dominate the pass-succession and possession tables, consistently keeping the club in the mid-table positions. As a reward for his hard work, Rodgers signed a three-and-a-half year contract extension in February 2011 to keep Brendan at the club until 2015. Swansea later defeated Liverpool 1-0 at the Liberty Stadium on the final day of the season, securing a respectable 11th place finish in the process.

Liverpool

After a disappointing league campaign under Kenny Dalglish, Liverpool opted to change managers in the summer of 2012.

Impressed with Brendan Rodgers' tactical knowledge, motivating skills and progressive philosophy, Fenway Sports Group instantly sought out Rodgers to elevate the club back into the Champions League spots. Upon interview, Rodgers unveiled a 180-page dossier, meticulously detailing the strategy of how to get Liverpool back to the pinnacle of English football. The owners, clearly impressed with Rodgers strategic planning, awarded him with a three-year contract on July 1, 2012.

At Brendan's unveiling, he instantly stuck a chord with the Reds' fan base. Rodgers vowed to fight for the club and its principles, both on and off the field, to implement attractive and offensive football and that he would leave 'no stone unturned' to get Liverpool back on the European map again. Shortly after, Rodgers and his family were shown around his new home stadium, where he immediately suggested that the club change the renowned 'This is Anfield' sign to its former design and to reintroduce the infamous red nets in goal.

In iconic fashion, Rodgers made it clear that the club needed to return to its traditional and successful roots.

Having seized one of the biggest jobs in world football, Rodgers showed that he had learned from his failings at Reading by refusing to guarantee the future of Andy Carroll, Liverpool's lacklustre £35 million signing who only flourished under a direct style of play. Shortly after, relics of Dalglish's team such as Charlie Adam Carroll himself made way for new signings Joe Allen and Fabio Borini. Allen had been heralded as being 'the engine' to Rodgers' Swansea side, while Borini had worked under the manager at both Chelsea and Swansea. With both players possessing strong technical abilities and the capacity to play a variety of roles in Rodgers' preferred 4-3-3 system, there was a clear paradigm shift in the make-up of the squad.

After a shaky introduction to life at Liverpool, with a haphazard transfer window, the BEING: documentary and zero victories in the opening five fixtures, Rodgers was quick to engage with fans to underline his vision, beliefs and values. A month into the season, Rodgers spoke to This Is Anfield and the other support groups, vowing to bring the opposition a 'death by football' in the long-term, whilst also recognising the uncertainty that must linger around the support. Never before had a Liverpool manager engaged with the fans so directly and so insightfully.

Since then, Rodgers' Liverpool side have gone from strength to strength.

Key players have emerged and been improved: Luis Suarez looks revitalised in the offensive-minded team set-up, showing the world-class abilities the striker had always shown promise of delivering, whilst Raheem Sterling, a young prospect with a lot of talent, became a first team starter after a series of disappointing performances from Stewart Downing.

The additions of Philippe Coutinho and Daniel Sturridge truly bought Brendan Rodgers' ambitions into reality, with the team increasingly becoming accustomed to not only a passing style but also one which works harder off the ball and produces a higher frequency of goalscoring chances. Stalemates at home had become a habit under Kenny Dalglish and Roy Hodgson, but Brendan Rodgers has slowly built up Anfield to a fortress it once was, sweeping aside minnows in regular fashion.

A mere two years after Rodgers was appointed, Liverpool have now finished runners-up in a hotly contested Premier League season, scoring over 100 goals, racking up 84 points and bringing Champions League football back to Anfield.

Rodgers has emerged from his humble beginnings and tribulations to cement himself into Liverpool folklore, driving the club's first substantial title challenge in a generation. His side not only play the most attractive football seen at Anfield for decades, but the manager himself has an aura of class and dignity around his work which the fans, and the media, respond well to. In short, Rodgers has brought the club back closer toward the Liverpool Way and encapsulates this philosophy in all facets of his management.

With the "framework" in place of a contract which will extend Brendan Rodgers' stay at Liverpool until 2018, here's hoping that Rodgers will be a mainstay the club for years to come, bringing silverware and glory along the way.

15. Under-21s and under-18s Academy review

By Ben Twelves

Liverpool's youth and development teams continued to flourish in the club's ever-evolving set-up, with both sides enjoying plenty of positives from a campaign where the only missing ingredient was silverware.

Under-21s boss Alex Inglethorpe guided his side to a second-placed finish in the Premier League, qualifying for the end of season play-offs which, sadly, ended prematurely at the semi-final stage for the second year running. While not the ending that the young Reds wanted, the team's achievement does show a real consistency from a side that has been chopped and changed almost weekly and the boss deserves praise for his work this campaign.

The 21s produced some fantastic football and ended the season with the highest amount of goals scored in the division, bagging 55 in just 21 games. Goals bring wins, and Inglethorpe's men picked up their fair share along the way, including impressive victories such as a 5-0 thrashing of Tottenham, a 4-2 win over Manchester United and a 5-2 victory against Newcastle United. The similarities between the first team and the younger sides again becomes apparent in the mentality and attack-minded prowess of the 21s.

Jack Dunn finished as the Reds' top scorer, notching an impressive 10 goals in 18 games and will no doubt be pushing for first team recognition next season, having made a fleeting goalscoring appearance in the end-of-season friendly against Shamrock Rovers. Portuguese playmaker Joao Teixeira proved an influential figure during his 13 appearances, scoring five goals in the process. Left-sided player Brad Smith, who made his debut for Brendan Rodgers' first team against Chelsea in December 2013, experienced a good season, claiming five assists and two goals while featuring in a number of positions. Though usually a full-back, he operated further forward in midfield and also as the right-sided attacker in a front three.

Honourable mentions must go to the senior squad members such as goalkeeper Danny Ward, whose calm and collected performances earned him international recognition with Wales under-21s, and tricky winger Kristoffer Peterson, whose six goals in 14 games prompted local League One side Tranmere Rovers to turn the Swede for help in their relegation battle. Powerful right-back Ryan McLaughlin carried on his career development, making the jump from the 21s side to enjoying a loan spell in the Championship with Barnsley, where he made nine appearances. Spanish centre-back Rafael Paez enjoyed a strong debut campaign, proving a calming influence in the back four, while Jordan Lussey too had a productive season in central midfield.

A highlight of the campaign was undoubtedly the return to action for American Marc Pelosi, who had been out for 14 months after suffering a nasty leg break.

The gradual track of progression toward first team action that continues to be provided for the aspiring youngsters has been extremely positive too. Youth team players Cameron Brannagan and Lloyd Jones have featured heavily for the 21s side, racking up 39 appearances between them and displaying maturity beyond their years—and let's not forget academy player of the year, Jordan Rossiter, who alongside recording 21 appearances has also received first team recognition season with a place on the bench in two matches.

For Neil Critchley's young scholars, the under-18 Premier League campaign saw a third-place finish in the North division, meaning they missed out on making the end of season play-off competition. There was also heartbreak at the quarter final stage of the FA Youth Cup for the Reds, losing out on penalties to Reading after a mammoth encounter finished 4-4 after extra time. Even so, there were a number of excellent performances and results throughout the campaign including a 5-0 thumping of West Ham United and 3-1 wins over rivals Manchester United and Everton.

While the youngsters didn't reap the rewards of their hard work with medals, their performances were repaid in trust and progression to under-21 team involvement, where the budding professionals gained some invaluable experience. Captain Connor Randall and fellow full-back Joe Maguire were two of the recipients and both rose to the challenge, showing their quality against players years older than they. The versatile Jordan Williams joined the two defenders in contributing well for both teams.

Productive seasons were played out by Daniel Cleary, whose comfort in possession and aggression in defence made him an integral part of the youth team in his 16 appearances, and Alex O'Hanlon, who produced consistent performances all season despite playing a number of positions on the left side.

Elsewhere, Spanish playmaker Pedro Chirivella captained the under-17s to Milk Cup glory in August 2013 and the technical midfielder showed real quality in keeping the team ticking over with his intelligent use of the ball during the league season.

A whole host of attacking talent filled the under-18 squad, which included the outstanding Harry Wilson—who became the clubs youngest ever international after he received a first cap for Wales in October 2013. Intelligent playmaker Daniel Trickett-Smith is another hot prospect and he, along with fleet-footed winger Sheyi Ojo and the creative Ryan Kent, formed an incredibly exciting attack which saw the Reds score 69 goals. Highly rated striker Jerome Sinclair finished the side's top scorer despite a spell out injured, notching 11 goals in 22 games.

The future certainly looks bright for Liverpool, with the academy continuing to nurture and produce some top talents who will be looking to follow in the footsteps of first team regulars Jon Flanagan and Raheem Sterling next season. First team boss Brendan Rodgers has continually shown his faith in the club's young prospects, and what an incentive it must be for the academy players to continue their good work knowing they may just be handed the chance they crave in senior football.

On that score, one final nod of appreciation should go to both Rodgers and the youngsters he entrusted with first-team duty in the end-of-season friendly in Dublin: McLaughlin, Paez, Smith,

Brannagan, Teixeira, Randall, Williams, Peterson and Dunn all featured in the 4-0 win over Shamrock Rovers. While some may look to gain loan experience next season, or continue their progression through the Reds' own youth ranks, being involved with the first-team scene can only bode well for their futures. Pre-season will be another opportunity for some, and supporters could feasibly get rather more acquainted with several of those youngsters next season.

16. Liverpool Loan Watch

By Jack Lusby

It is generally believed to be an advantage for a young player from a Premier League side to spend a development spell on loan at a lower-level club, something the Reds have utilised to good (and not-so-good) effect in previous campaigns. This season, several of the Reds' young prospects have spent all or part of the campaign away from the club to further their experience in the game.

At home...

Particularly impressive have been the contributions of Fabio Borini and Oussama Assaidi, on loan at Sunderland and Stoke City respectively, as they have shown they can handle the pressures of the Premier League on a regular basis. In fact, the pair played their own part in Liverpool's title challenge with both scoring vital winners against Chelsea. Borini featured 32 times in the league for the Black Cats, scoring seven goals and providing two assists along the way. He most frequently operated from the left side of the attack, but played centrally on occasion too. Borini also netted Sunderland's goal in the League Cup final at Wembley. Assaidi, meanwhile, made 19 appearances for Stoke in the league, 12 of them from the start. He scored four goals but, despite creating 19 chances, did not claim an assist.

Further down the league ladder, Jordon Ibe (Birmingham City),

Ryan McLaughlin (Barnsley), Andre Wisdom (Derby County), Jack Robinson (Blackpool) and Conor Coady (Sheffield United) have all impressed given regular game time. Ibe scored one in his 11 Championship appearances with the Blues, while right-back McLaughlin played nine times for Barnsley, spending a shorter periods with those club than the other youngsters did with theirs.

Wisdom gained over 3,000 minutes of game time in his 36 appearances for Derby, playing from full-back, while Robinson wasn't far off that with 34 games. Coady made 39 appearances as Sheffield United just missed out on the League One play-offs, with the midfielder scoring five goals along the way, but he was also heavily involved in their FA Cup run and played at Wembley in their semi-final fixture.

Less impressive have been the loan spells of Joao Carlos Teixeira at Brentford and Michael Ngoo at Yeovil Town and Walsall. Teixeira lasted a month at the west London club, making two appearances, while Ngoo has struggled to find the net at either of his loan clubs this season. Ngoo scored one in a total of 20 league appearances between the two loan spells.

...and abroad

Meanwhile, some of the Reds' more high-profile names have spent temporary spells abroad, to varying degrees of success.

Following his public flirtation with a move to Spanish giants Barcelona, the fate of Pepe Reina under the stewardship of Rodgers looked to be bleak indeed. The Spaniard was swiftly loaned to Rafa Benitez's Napoli following the signing of Simon Mignolet, where Reina made 30 league appearances, helping his side to a third-place finish in Serie A.

Summer signing Tiago Ilori spent the second half of the season at Spanish side Granada. The Portuguese centre-back only made nine La Liga appearances during his time at the relegation battlers, partly due to injury, but performed admirably, including a superlative display marking Lionel Messi in April's surprise 1-0 victory over Barcelona. Spanish playmaker Suso also spent the season in La Liga with fellow strugglers Almeria, and impressed hugely in spells with three goals—including a superb curling free-kick against Espanyol—and seven assists in 33 appearances; Almeria finished 17th in the league table having survived the drop with a 0-0 draw on the final day. Suso was not involved that match, being an unused sub.

Elsewhere, youngster Krisztian Adorjan scored three goals and claimed one assist at Dutch Eredivisie side FC Gronigen, though they have opted not to make the move permanent. Uruguayan central defender Seb Coates spent several months with Nacional in his home country, where he featured half a dozen times after recovering from a long-term knee injury, enough to force his way back into the national team squad ahead of the World Cup in Brazil.

The Future

After impressing at Sunderland, Borini will likely return to supplement the strike talents of Luis Suarez and Daniel Sturridge, whilst Ibe, McLaughlin, Wisdom, Robinson, Ilori and Suso will flesh out the Reds' squad significantly for a rigorous 2014-15 campaign—Wisdom and Ilori in particular could have their sights on first-team places.

On their way out, however, it is likely that Anfield has seen the last of Assaidi, Coady, Ngoo, Adorjan and Coates and will also have said goodbye to the long-serving Reina, with the goalkeeper unlikely to regain his place in the first-team over Mignolet.

17. LFC Premier League statistics of 2013-14

Appearances (total)
1. Simon Mignolet – 38
2. Martin Skrtel – 36
3. Jordan Henderson – 35
4. Steven Gerrard – 34
=5. Raheem Sterling, Luis Suarez, Philippe Coutinho - 33

Substitute appearances
1. Victor Moses – 13
=2. Raheem Sterling, Joe Allen, Iago Aspas, Luis Alberto - 9

Goals
1. Luis Suarez – 31
2. Daniel Sturridge -21
3. Steven Gerrard – 13
4. Raheem Sterling – 9
5. Martin Skrtel - 7

Yellow cards
1. Steven Gerrard – 7
=2. Luis Suarez, Martin Skrtel, Lucas Leiva – 6
=5. Jordan Henderson; Joe Allen - 4

Red cards
1. Jordan Henderson - 1

Printed in Great Britain
by Amazon.co.uk, Ltd.,
Marston Gate.